ATKINS DIET COOKBOOK

A complete Tasty and Effortless Guide to sustainable weight loss and Healthy Eating

ROWENA .M. LEE

INTRODUCTION

Welcome to the Atkins Diet Cookbook your ultimate companion on the journey to a healthier, more vibrant you! If you're seeking to embrace a lifestyle change, shed those unwanted pounds, or simply explore the exciting world of lowcarb eating, you've stumbled upon the perfect resource. This book is a comprehensive guide to the renowned Atkins Diet, a revolutionary nutritional approach that has transformed the lives of countless individuals worldwide.

The Atkins Diet is a lowcarbohydrate, highfat, and moderateprotein diet that focuses on achieving a metabolic state known as ketosis. By limiting your carbohydrate intake and increasing your consumption of healthy fats and proteins, your body transitions from burning glucose (from carbs) for energy to efficiently burning fat instead. This remarkable metabolic shift not only aids in sustainable weight loss but also offers a myriad of additional benefits, such as improved energy levels, enhanced mental clarity, and a reduced risk of chronic diseases.

However, the Atkins Diet is much more than just a weightloss strategy; it's a holistic lifestyle change that emphasizes the importance of making informed food choices and maintaining a balanced, nutrientdense diet. Throughout this meticulously crafted cookbook, you'll discover a treasure trove of delectable and satisfying recipes that seamlessly align with the principles of the Atkins Diet, ensuring that you never have to sacrifice flavor or nutrition on your journey to better health.

Before we dive into the mouthwatering recipes, let's explore the fundamental principles that underpin the Atkins Diet. This innovative approach is divided into four distinct phases, each carefully designed to guide you through a gradual transition into a sustainable lowcarb lifestyle while simultaneously helping you achieve your desired health and weight goals.

The induction phase, which typically lasts two weeks, kickstarts the process of ketosis by limiting your daily carbohydrate intake to 20 grams or less. During this phase, you'll focus on consuming highfat, highprotein foods, such as meats, eggs, cheese, and healthy oils, while avoiding most carbohydrate sources like grains, fruits, and starchy vegetables.

As you progress through the subsequent phases, you'll gradually increase your carbohydrate intake by reintroducing nutrientdense, lowcarb vegetables and a limited amount of fruits into your diet. The goal is to find your personal carbohydrate tolerance level – the sweet spot that allows you to continue losing weight at a steady and sustainable pace while experiencing the myriad benefits of a lowcarb lifestyle.

One of the key principles that sets the Atkins Diet apart is the concept of "net carbs." Net carbs are calculated by subtracting the grams of fiber from the total grams of carbohydrates in a food item. This innovative approach recognizes that fiber is not fully digested and absorbed by the body, making it less impactful on blood sugar levels and ketosis. By focusing on net carbs instead of total carbohydrates, you'll be able to enjoy a wider variety of lowcarb, fiberrich foods while still adhering to the principles of the Atkins Diet.

Throughout this cookbook, you'll not only find a diverse array of delectable recipes but also practical tips, personal experiences, and valuable insights from individuals who have successfully embraced the Atkins Diet lifestyle. These reallife stories and strategies will inspire, motivate, and provide you with a deeper understanding of how to navigate the challenges and overcome obstacles that may arise along your lowcarb journey.

Explanation of the LowCarb, HighFat Approach

At the core of the Atkins Diet lies a revolutionary approach to nutrition – a lowcarbohydrate, highfat, and moderateprotein way of eating that challenges conventional dietary wisdom. This unique approach is designed to induce a metabolic state known as ketosis, wherein your body shifts from relying on glucose as its primary fuel source to efficiently burning fat for energy.

To fully grasp the transformative power of this approach, it's essential to understand the intricate relationship between carbohydrates, fats, and the body's energy systems. Carbohydrates, which are readily converted into glucose, have long been touted as the body's preferred energy source. However, when carbohydrate intake is drastically reduced, as in the case of the Atkins Diet, the body is forced to seek an alternative fuel source – and that's where fat comes into play.

By limiting your carbohydrate consumption and increasing your intake of healthy fats and moderate amounts of protein, you essentially "reprogram" your metabolism to enter a state of ketosis. In this metabolic state, the liver begins to convert fatty acids into ketone bodies, which serve as an efficient and sustainable source of energy for the brain, heart, and other vital organs.

The beauty of this lowcarb, highfat approach lies in its ability to promote sustainable weight loss while also offering a host of additional benefits. By relying on fat as your primary fuel source, your body becomes more efficient at burning stored body fat, leading to a reduction in overall body weight and improved body composition.

Moreover, ketosis has been shown to have a positive impact on various aspects of health, including improved cognitive function, enhanced energy levels, and better management of certain chronic conditions, such as type 2 diabetes and epilepsy. When in ketosis, many individuals report experiencing a heightened sense of mental clarity, focus, and overall wellbeing.

One of the key advantages of the lowcarb, highfat approach is its ability to promote a feeling of satiety and curb cravings. By consuming nutrientdense, highfat foods like avocados, nuts, seeds, and healthy oils, you'll experience a greater sense of fullness and satisfaction, which can help reduce the temptation to overeat or indulge in unhealthy snacking.

Additionally, the highfat aspect of this approach encourages the consumption of nutrientrich, whole foods that are often overlooked or demonized in traditional diets. Foods like fatty fish, avocados, and fullfat dairy products not only provide essential nutrients but also offer a delightful array of flavors and textures that can enhance your overall eating experience.

It's important to note that not all fats are created equal, and the Atkins Diet emphasizes the importance of choosing healthy, unsaturated fats from sources such as avocados, olive oil, nuts, and fatty fish. These fats are not only beneficial for overall health but also play a crucial role in supporting the body's transition into ketosis and maintaining this metabolic state.

By embracing the lowcarb, highfat approach, you'll embark on a transformative journey that not only supports weight loss but also promotes overall health and wellbeing. As you delve deeper into this cookbook, you'll discover a world of delectable recipes that seamlessly incorporate this revolutionary nutritional philosophy, allowing you to indulge in flavorful and satisfying meals while achieving your desired health and wellness goals.

Importance of Maintaining a Balanced Diet

While the Atkins Diet emphasizes a lowcarbohydrate, highfat approach, it's crucial to remember that achieving optimal health and wellbeing goes beyond merely adhering to macronutrient ratios. True wellness is a harmonious symphony, and maintaining a balanced diet plays a pivotal role in ensuring that your body receives the nourishment it needs to thrive.

At the heart of the Atkins Diet lies a commitment to nutrientdensity – a philosophy that champions the consumption of whole, unprocessed foods that are rich in essential vitamins, minerals, antioxidants, and other vital compounds. By prioritizing nutrientdense choices, you not only support your body's transition into ketosis but also provide it with the building blocks necessary for overall health and vitality.

One of the remarkable advantages of a wellformulated lowcarb, highfat diet is its ability to naturally promote the consumption of a diverse array of nutrientrich foods. From vibrant leafy greens and colorful vegetables to healthy fats, highquality proteins, and lowglycemic fruits, the Atkins Diet encourages you to explore a vast culinary landscape brimming with flavor and nourishment.

Throughout this cookbook, you'll find a meticulously curated collection of recipes that not only adhere to the principles of the Atkins Diet but also celebrate the beauty of whole, minimally processed ingredients. Each dish is a harmonious symphony of flavors, textures, and nutrients, designed to nourish your body and soul while satisfying your taste buds.

Maintaining a balanced diet on the Atkins Diet extends beyond simply meeting your macronutrient needs. It involves embracing a holistic approach that considers the intricate interplay between various vitamins, minerals, and phytonutrients, and how they collectively contribute to your overall health and wellbeing.

By incorporating a diverse range of nutrientdense foods into your meals, you'll not only support your body's nutritional requirements but also reap the benefits of synergistic interactions between these vital compounds. For instance, the combination of healthy fats and fatsoluble vitamins, such as vitamins A, D, E, and K, can enhance their absorption and utilization within the body.

Moreover, a balanced diet rich in antioxidants, fiber, and antiinflammatory compounds can help mitigate the potential risks associated with any dietary approach, including the Atkins Diet. By prioritizing nutrientdense choices, you'll be providing your body with the tools it needs to combat oxidative stress, support a healthy gut microbiome, and reduce inflammation – all of which contribute to overall wellbeing and longevity.

It's important to note that maintaining a balanced diet is not a onesizefitsall endeavor. Every individual has unique nutritional needs, preferences, and health considerations. Throughout this cookbook, you'll find practical tips and guidance on how to tailor your lowcarb, highfat journey to your specific requirements, ensuring that you're nourishing your body in a way that aligns with your personal goals and circumstances.

By embracing the principles of a balanced, nutrientdense diet within the framework of the Atkins Diet, you'll embark on a transformative journey that transcends mere weight loss. You'll cultivate a deeper appreciation for the nourishing power of whole, minimally processed foods, and discover a newfound vitality that permeates every aspect of your life. So, let's embark on this culinary adventure together, where flavor, nutrition, and wellbeing converge in perfect harmony.

CHAPTER ONE: UNDERSTANDING THE ATKINS DIET

The Atkins Diet is not merely a fleeting trend or a quickfix solution; it's a comprehensive lifestyle change that has withstood the test of time, empowering countless individuals to take control of their health and wellbeing. At its core, this revolutionary approach to nutrition challenges conventional dietary wisdom by embracing a lowcarbohydrate, highfat, and moderateprotein way of eating.

As someone who has personally experienced the transformative power of the Atkins Diet, I can attest to the profound impact it has had on my life. What began as a decision to shed a few extra pounds quickly evolved into a journey of selfdiscovery, where I learned to listen to my body's innate wisdom and cultivate a deeper appreciation for nutrientdense, whole foods.

One of the key principles that sets the Atkins Diet apart is its ability to induce a metabolic state known as ketosis. By drastically reducing your carbohydrate intake and increasing your consumption of healthy fats and moderate amounts of protein, your body is forced to seek an alternative fuel source – and that's where the magic happens. Your liver begins to convert fatty acids into ketone bodies, which serve as an efficient and sustainable energy source for your brain, heart, and other vital organs.

As I embarked on my own lowcarb journey, I was initially apprehensive about the dietary changes required to achieve ketosis. However, as I delved deeper into the Atkins Diet phases and embraced the concept of net carbs, a world of culinary possibilities unfolded before me. I discovered that by focusing on the net carb content of foods – the total carbohydrates minus the fiber – I could enjoy a diverse array of nutrientdense, fiberrich foods while still adhering to the principles of a ketogenic lifestyle.

One of the remarkable benefits I experienced while in ketosis was a heightened sense of mental clarity and focus. Gone were the midday energy slumps and brain fog; instead, I found myself feeling alert and productive throughout the day. This newfound cognitive clarity allowed me to tackle tasks with renewed vigor and approach challenges with a sharper, more focused mindset.

Moreover, the Atkins Diet's emphasis on nutrientdensity ensured that I was nourishing my body with a wealth of essential vitamins, minerals, and antioxidants. By prioritizing whole, minimally processed foods like leafy greens, fatty fish, avocados, and nuts, I was not only satisfying my cravings but also providing my body with the building blocks it needed to thrive.

As I progressed through the phases of the Atkins Diet, I learned the importance of listening to my body's cues and adapting my approach accordingly. Each phase offered its own unique challenges and rewards, but by remaining attuned to how different foods affected my energy levels, cravings, and overall wellbeing, I was able to make informed choices that supported my longterm success.

The Atkins Diet is not a rigid set of rules or a onesizefitsall approach; rather, it's a flexible framework that empowers you to take control of your health and wellbeing. By understanding the phases, embracing the concept of net carbs, and armed with comprehensive food lists, you'll be wellequipped to embark on a transformative journey towards better health, sustainable weight loss, and a lifetime of culinary delights.

Phases of the Atkins Diet

At the heart of the Atkins Diet lies a structured, multiphased approach that guides you through a gradual and sustainable transition into a lowcarb lifestyle. Each phase is meticulously designed to support your body's adaptation to burning fat for fuel while providing the flexibility to find your personal carbohydrate tolerance level.

Phase 1: Induction

The induction phase serves as the catalyst for your lowcarb transformation, kickstarting the process of ketosis and setting the stage for remarkable metabolic changes. During this initial twoweek period, you'll limit your daily carbohydrate intake to a strict 20 grams or less, primarily derived from nutrientdense, lowcarb vegetables.

As someone who has navigated the induction phase firsthand, I can attest to the sheer power of this initial stage. While the carbohydrate restriction may seem daunting at first, the rapid results and the array of delectable food choices quickly make it a worthwhile endeavor. From savory baconwrapped chicken breasts to creamy avocado deviled eggs, the induction phase offers a diverse culinary landscape that will tantalize your taste buds while supporting your body's transition into ketosis.

Phase 2: Ongoing Weight Loss

Once you've successfully completed the induction phase and experienced the benefits of ketosis, you'll transition into the ongoing weight loss phase. During this phase, you'll gradually increase your carbohydrate intake by reintroducing nutrientdense, lowcarb vegetables and a limited amount of fruits back into your diet.

The key to success in this phase lies in finding your personal carbohydrate tolerance level – the sweet spot that allows you to continue losing weight at a steady and sustainable pace while enjoying the benefits of a lowcarb lifestyle. This process involves carefully monitoring your body's response to the addition of specific food groups and adjusting your carbohydrate intake accordingly.

Throughout my own journey, I discovered that the ongoing weight loss phase offered a newfound sense of flexibility and variety in my meal planning. By strategically incorporating nutrientrich veggies like leafy greens, bell peppers, and zucchini, I was able to craft flavorful and satisfying dishes that kept me feeling full and energized, without compromising my progress.

Phase 3: PreMaintenance

As you approach your target weight and begin to see the remarkable results of your efforts, you'll enter the premaintenance phase. During this phase, you'll continue to gradually increase your carbohydrate intake, adding more nutrientdense carbs to your diet while closely monitoring your body's response.

The objective of the premaintenance phase is to find the carbohydrate level that allows you to maintain your desired weight while still experiencing the benefits of a lowcarb lifestyle. This phase is characterized by a greater degree of flexibility, enabling you to incorporate a wider variety of foods while remaining mindful of portion control and macronutrient balance.

Phase 4: Lifetime Maintenance

The final phase, lifetime maintenance, is a testament to the transformative power of the Atkins Diet. By this stage, you'll have successfully established your personal carbohydrate tolerance level and learned how to maintain a healthy, balanced, and sustainable lowcarb lifestyle.

During the lifetime maintenance phase, you'll have the freedom to incorporate a wider range of foods into your diet, while still prioritizing nutrientdense, whole foods that support your overall health and wellbeing. This phase encourages mindful eating habits and allows for occasional indulgences, empowering you to savor life's culinary pleasures without sacrificing your hardearned progress.

One of the most valuable lessons I learned throughout the phases of the Atkins Diet was the importance of patience, selfawareness, and adaptability. Each phase presented its own unique challenges and triumphs, but by remaining attuned to my body's cues and adjusting my approach accordingly, I was able to navigate the journey with confidence and achieve lasting success.

Explanation of Net Carbs

At the core of the Atkins Diet lies a revolutionary concept that has transformed the way we approach carbohydrate consumption: net carbs. This groundbreaking approach recognizes that not all carbohydrates are created equal and introduces a more nuanced understanding of how different types of carbs impact our bodies.

Net carbs are calculated by subtracting the grams of fiber from the total grams of carbohydrates in a food item. This deduction is based on the simple fact that fiber, a type of indigestible carbohydrate, is not fully absorbed and metabolized by the body, making it less impactful on blood sugar levels and the state of ketosis.

As someone who has embraced the concept of net carbs, I can attest to the profound impact it has had on my relationship with food and my overall dietary experience. Prior to discovering this principle, I found myself unnecessarily restricting nutrientdense, fiberrich foods like leafy greens, cruciferous vegetables, and nuts, out of fear that their carbohydrate content would derail my progress.

However, by focusing on net carbs instead of total carbohydrates, a whole new world of culinary possibilities opened up before me. Suddenly, I could enjoy the rich flavors and textures of foods that were once offlimits, without compromising my commitment to a lowcarb lifestyle.

One of the most remarkable benefits of the net carb approach is its ability to promote overall digestive health and wellbeing. By prioritizing fiberrich foods, I was not only supporting my body's transition into ketosis but also nourishing my gut microbiome and promoting regular bowel movements – a crucial aspect of overall health that is often overlooked.

As I delved deeper into the world of net carbs, I discovered that certain foods, like avocados, olives, and nuts, which were once considered high in carbohydrates, could now be enjoyed in moderation thanks to their impressive fiber content. These nutrientdense powerhouses quickly became staples in my diet, adding a delightful array of flavors and textures to my meals while keeping me feeling satiated and energized.

Moreover, the net carb concept allowed me to indulge in the occasional treat without completely derailing my progress. By carefully tracking my net carb intake and making mindful choices, I could savor a small portion of dark chocolate or a few fresh berries without the guilt or fear of sabotaging my efforts.

It's important to note that while the net carb approach offers greater flexibility and variety, it still requires diligence and moderation. Not all foods with a low net carb count are created equal, and it's crucial to prioritize nutrientdense, whole foods over processed options.

By embracing the concept of net carbs, I was able to cultivate a more sustainable and enjoyable approach to lowcarb living. It allowed me to nourish my body with a diverse array of flavors and textures while still adhering to the principles of the Atkins Diet. As you embark on your own lowcarb journey, understanding and implementing the net carb principle will undoubtedly be a gamechanger, empowering you to make informed choices and savor every delicious bite.

Food Lists for Each Phase

Navigating the phases of the Atkins Diet can be a delicious and rewarding journey, but having a comprehensive understanding of the recommended and restricted foods for each stage is crucial for success. These carefully curated food lists serve as your roadmap, empowering you to make informed choices and nourish your body with nutrientdense, satisfying meals that align with the principles of a lowcarb lifestyle.

Phase 1: Induction

During the induction phase, when your body is embarking on its transition into ketosis, the focus is on consuming highfat, highprotein foods while strictly limiting your carbohydrate intake to 20 grams or less of net carbs per day. This initial phase lays the foundation for your lowcarb journey, and the food list reflects this. Meats, eggs, cheese, healthy fats like avocado and olive oil, and nutrientdense, lowcarb veggies like leafy greens, cucumbers, and bell peppers will become your culinary companions.

As someone who has navigated the induction phase, I can attest to the abundance of delectable options available. From savory baconwrapped chicken breasts to creamy avocado deviled eggs, this phase offers a diverse array of flavors and textures that will tantalize your taste buds while supporting your body's metabolic shift.

Phase 2: Ongoing Weight Loss

Once you've successfully completed the induction phase and experienced the benefits of ketosis, you'll transition into the ongoing weight loss phase. During this stage, you'll gradually increase your carbohydrate intake by reintroducing nutrientdense, lowcarb vegetables and a limited amount of berries and lowcarb fruits back into your diet.

The food list for this phase builds upon the foundation established in the induction phase, expanding your culinary horizons while still prioritizing nutrientdense, whole foods. In addition to the foods allowed in Phase 1, you'll now be able to enjoy a wider variety of lowcarb veggies like broccoli, cauliflower, and zucchini, as well as a moderate amount of nuts and seeds.

Phase 3: PreMaintenance

As you approach your target weight and begin to see the remarkable results of your efforts, you'll enter the premaintenance phase. During this stage, you'll continue to gradually increase your carbohydrate intake, adding more nutrientdense carbs to your diet while closely monitoring your body's response.

The food list for the premaintenance phase reflects this increased flexibility, allowing you to incorporate a wider range of foods while still adhering to the principles of a lowcarb lifestyle. In addition to the foods permitted in the previous phases, you'll now be able to enjoy additional lowcarb fruits like melon and citrus, as well as whole grains and legumes in moderation.

Phase 4: Lifetime Maintenance

The final phase, lifetime maintenance, is a celebration of the transformative power of the Atkins Diet. By this stage, you'll have successfully established your personal carbohydrate tolerance level and learned how to maintain a healthy, balanced, and sustainable lowcarb lifestyle.

During the lifetime maintenance phase, the food list embraces a balanced variety of nutrientdense foods from all food groups. The emphasis remains on whole, minimally processed foods that nourish your body and support your overall wellbeing. While there is greater flexibility in this phase, it's still important to prioritize foods that align with your personal goals and avoid those that trigger cravings or adverse reactions.

Throughout my own journey, these food lists have served as invaluable resources, guiding me through each phase with clarity and confidence. They not only provided me with a framework for making informed choices but also opened my eyes to the vast array of delicious and satisfying options available within the lowcarb lifestyle.

Remember, these food lists are meant to serve as general guidelines, and individual experiences may vary. It's crucial to listen to your body's cues and adapt your approach accordingly. Additionally, consulting with a healthcare professional can help ensure that your dietary choices align with your specific needs and any underlying medical conditions.

By embracing the power of these comprehensive food lists, you'll be wellequipped to navigate the phases of the Atkins Diet with ease, unlocking a world of culinary delights that will tantalize your taste buds while supporting your health and wellness goals.

Veggie Egg Muffins

Prep: 10 mins | Cook: 20 mins | Serves: 6 muffins

Ingredients:
- 6 large eggs
- 1/4 cup chopped bell peppers (US) / 60g chopped bell peppers (UK)
- 1/4 cup chopped spinach (US) / 60g chopped spinach (UK)
- 1/4 cup diced tomatoes (US) / 60g diced tomatoes (UK)
- Salt and pepper to taste

Instructions:
1. Preheat your oven to 350°F (175°C). Grease a muffin tin or line with muffin liners.
2. In a mixing bowl, whisk together eggs, bell peppers, spinach, tomatoes, salt, and pepper.
3. Pour the egg mixture evenly into the muffin cups, filling each about 2/3 full.
4. Bake for 1520 minutes or until the muffins are set and slightly golden on top.
5. Remove from the oven and let cool for a few minutes before serving.
6. Enjoy these veggie egg muffins warm or store them in an airtight container in the refrigerator for up to 3 days.

Nutritional Info (per muffin): Calories: 80 | Fat: 5g | Carbs: 2g | Protein: 7g

Atkins Diet Feature: Low in carbs, high in protein, and packed with veggies for a nutritious breakfast option.

Turkey Bacon Egg Cups

Prep: 10 mins | Cook: 20 mins | Serves: 4 cups

Ingredients:
- 4 slices turkey bacon
- 4 large eggs
- Salt and pepper to taste
- Chopped chives for garnish (optional)

Instructions:
1. Preheat your oven to 375°F (190°C). Lightly grease four cups of a muffin tin.
2. Wrap each slice of turkey bacon around the sides of each muffin cup, creating a cup shape.
3. Crack an egg into each baconlined cup. Season with salt and pepper.
4. Bake in the preheated oven for 1520 minutes or until the egg whites are set.
5. Garnish with chopped chives if desired and serve hot.
6. These turkey bacon egg cups are great for a lowcarb, proteinpacked breakfast!

Nutritional Info (per cup): Calories: 120 | Fat: 8g | Carbs: 1g | Protein: 10g

Atkins Diet Feature: Low in carbs and high in protein, these egg cups are a satisfying breakfast choice.

Prep: 15 mins | Cook: 45 mins | Serves: 4

Ingredients:
- 6 eggs
- 1/2 cup heavy cream (US) / 120ml heavy cream (UK)
- 1 cup diced ham (US) / 150g diced ham (UK)
- 1 cup shredded cheddar cheese (US) / 100g shredded cheddar cheese (UK)
- Salt and pepper to taste

Instructions:
1. Preheat your oven to 375°F (190°C). Grease a baking dish.
2. In a mixing bowl, whisk together eggs, heavy cream, salt, and pepper.
3. Stir in diced ham and shredded cheddar cheese.
4. Pour the mixture into the prepared baking dish.
5. Bake for 4045 minutes or until the casserole is set and the top is golden brown.
6. Allow the casserole to cool for a few minutes before slicing and serving.
7. This ham and cheese breakfast casserole is perfect for meal prep and can be reheated throughout the week.

Nutritional Info (per serving): Calories: 380 | Fat: 30g | Carbs: 2g | Protein: 24g

Atkins Diet Feature: High in protein and low in carbs, this casserole will keep you satisfied until your next meal.

Sausage and Egg Bake

Prep: 15 mins | Cook: 30 mins | Serves: 4

Ingredients:
- 8 oz breakfast sausage (US) / 225g breakfast sausage (UK)
- 6 large eggs
- 1/4 cup heavy cream (US) / 60ml heavy cream (UK)
- 1/2 cup shredded mozzarella cheese (US) / 50g shredded mozzarella cheese (UK)
- Salt and pepper to taste
- Chopped parsley for garnish (optional)

Instructions:
1. Preheat your oven to 375°F (190°C). Grease a baking dish.
2. Cook the breakfast sausage in a skillet over medium heat until browned and cooked through. Drain any excess fat.
3. In a mixing bowl, whisk together eggs, heavy cream, salt, and pepper.
4. Stir in cooked sausage and shredded mozzarella cheese.
5. Pour the mixture into the prepared baking dish.
6. Bake for 2530 minutes or until the bake is set and the top is lightly golden.
7. Garnish with chopped parsley if desired and serve hot.
8. This sausage and egg bake is a hearty and flavorful breakfast option, perfect for the Atkins Diet.

Nutritional Info (per serving): Calories: 320 | Fat: 25g | Carbs: 2g | Protein: 20g

Atkins Diet Feature: High in protein and low in carbs, this bake is a satisfying way to start your day.

Spinach Breakfast Quiche

Prep: 20 mins | Cook: 45 mins | Serves: 6

Ingredients:

- 1 unbaked lowcarb pie crust (storebought or homemade)
- 6 large eggs
- 1/2 cup heavy cream (US) / 120ml heavy cream (UK)
- 1 cup chopped spinach (US) / 100g chopped spinach (UK)
- 1/2 cup diced onions (US) / 75g diced onions (UK)
- 1/2 cup shredded Swiss cheese (US) / 50g shredded Swiss cheese (UK)
- Salt and pepper to taste

Instructions:

1. Preheat your oven to 375°F (190°C).
2. Line a pie dish with the unbaked lowcarb pie crust.
3. In a mixing bowl, whisk together eggs, heavy cream, salt, and pepper.
4. Stir in chopped spinach, diced onions, and shredded Swiss cheese.
5. Pour the mixture into the prepared pie crust.
6. Bake for 4045 minutes or until the quiche is set and the crust is golden brown.
7. Allow the quiche to cool for a few minutes before slicing and serving.
8. This spinach breakfast quiche is rich, creamy, and packed with flavor, making it a perfect Atkinsfriendly breakfast choice.

Nutritional Info (per serving): Calories: 280 | Fat: 20g | Carbs: 5g | Protein: 15g

Atkins Diet Feature: Low in carbs and high in protein, this quiche is a delicious way to enjoy your morning meal.

Prep: 10 mins | Cook: 10 mins | Serves: 2

Ingredients:
- 4 large eggs
- 1 cup chopped kale (US) / 100g chopped kale (UK)
- 1/2 cup shredded cheddar cheese (US) / 50g shredded cheddar cheese (UK)
- 2 tablespoons butter (US) / 30g butter (UK)
- Salt and pepper to taste

Instructions:
1. In a bowl, whisk together eggs, salt, and pepper until well combined.
2. Heat 1 tablespoon of butter in a nonstick skillet over medium heat.
3. Add chopped kale to the skillet and cook until wilted, about 23 minutes.
4. Pour half of the egg mixture into the skillet, swirling to spread evenly.
5. Cook the omelet for 23 minutes or until the edges start to set.
6. Sprinkle half of the shredded cheddar cheese over one half of the omelet.
7. Using a spatula, fold the other half of the omelet over the cheese.
8. Cook for another 12 minutes until the cheese is melted and the omelet is cooked through.
9. Repeat with the remaining ingredients to make the second omelet.
10. Serve the kale and cheese omelets hot, garnished with additional salt and pepper if desired.

Nutritional Info (per serving): Calories: 320 | Fat: 25g | Carbs: 3g | Protein: 18g

Atkins Diet Feature: Low in carbs and high in protein, these omelets are a nutritious and satisfying breakfast option.

Prep: 10 mins | Cook: 10 mins | Serves: 2

Ingredients:
- 4 large eggs
- 1/2 cup diced ham (US) / 75g diced ham (UK)
- 1/4 cup diced bell peppers (US) / 40g diced bell peppers (UK)
- 1/4 cup diced onions (US) / 40g diced onions (UK)
- 1/2 cup shredded mozzarella cheese (US) / 50g shredded mozzarella cheese (UK)
- 2 tablespoons butter (US) / 30g butter (UK)
- Salt and pepper to taste

Instructions:
1. In a bowl, whisk together eggs, salt, and pepper until well combined.
2. Heat 1 tablespoon of butter in a nonstick skillet over medium heat.
3. Add diced ham, bell peppers, and onions to the skillet and cook until softened, about 34 minutes.
4. Pour half of the egg mixture into the skillet, swirling to spread evenly.
5. Cook the omelet for 23 minutes or until the edges start to set.
6. Sprinkle half of the shredded mozzarella cheese over one half of the omelet.
7. Using a spatula, fold the other half of the omelet over the cheese.
8. Cook for another 12 minutes until the cheese is melted and the omelet is cooked through.
9. Repeat with the remaining ingredients to make the second omelet.
10. Serve the ham and veggie omelets hot, garnished with additional salt and pepper if desired.

Nutritional Info (per serving): Calories: 340 | Fat: 26g | Carbs: 3g | Protein: 21g

Atkins Diet Feature: High in protein and low in carbs, these omelets are a delicious and filling breakfast option.

Bacon, Egg, and Cheese Cups

Prep: 10 mins | Cook: 20 mins | Serves: 4 cups

Ingredients:
- 4 slices bacon
- 4 large eggs
- 1/2 cup shredded cheddar cheese (US) / 50g shredded cheddar cheese (UK)
- Salt and pepper to taste
- Chopped chives for garnish (optional)

Instructions:
1. Preheat your oven to 375°F (190°C). Grease four cups of a muffin tin.
2. Line each muffin cup with a slice of bacon, forming a cup shape.
3. Crack an egg into each baconlined cup. Season with salt and pepper.
4. Sprinkle shredded cheddar cheese over each egg.
5. Bake in the preheated oven for 1520 minutes or until the bacon is crispy and the egg whites are set.
6. Garnish with chopped chives if desired and serve hot.
7. These bacon, egg, and cheese cups are a satisfying and convenient breakfast option for the Atkins Diet.

Nutritional Info (per cup): Calories: 220 | Fat: 17g | Carbs: 1g | Protein: 15g

Atkins Diet Feature: Low in carbs and high in protein, these cups are perfect for a quick and easy breakfast on the go.

Prep: 5 mins | Cook: 10 mins | Serves: 2 sandwiches

Ingredients:
- 2 lowcarb English muffins, split
- 4 slices Canadian bacon
- 2 large eggs
- 2 slices cheddar cheese
- Salt and pepper to taste

Instructions:
1. Toast the English muffin halves until golden brown.
2. Heat a skillet over medium heat and lightly grease with cooking spray.
3. Cook the Canadian bacon slices in the skillet until heated through, about 2 minutes per side.
4. In the same skillet, crack the eggs and cook to your desired doneness, seasoning with salt and pepper.
5. Place a slice of Canadian bacon, a cooked egg, and a slice of cheddar cheese on the bottom half of each English muffin.
6. Top with the remaining English muffin halves to form sandwiches.
7. Serve the English muffin sandwiches immediately, optionally with hot sauce or ketchup.

Nutritional Info (per sandwich): Calories: 300 | Fat: 15g | Carbs: 15g | Protein: 25g

Atkins Diet Feature: Low in carbs and high in protein, these English muffin sandwiches are a delicious and filling breakfast choice.

Prep: 10 mins | Cook: 10 mins | Serves: 2

Ingredients:
- 2 slices lowcarb bread, toasted
- 1 ripe avocado
- 4 slices bacon, cooked until crispy
- 2 large eggs, cooked to your preference
- Salt and pepper to taste
- Red pepper flakes for garnish (optional)

Instructions:
1. Mash the ripe avocado in a bowl and season with salt and pepper.
2. Spread the mashed avocado evenly onto the toasted lowcarb bread slices.
3. Top each avocado toast with 2 slices of crispy bacon.
4. In the same skillet used to cook the bacon, fry the eggs to your desired doneness.
5. Carefully place a fried egg on top of each bacontopped avocado toast.
6. Garnish with red pepper flakes if desired, and serve immediately.

Nutritional Info (per serving): Calories: 350 | Fat: 25g | Carbs: 15g | Protein: 20g

Atkins Diet Feature: Packed with healthy fats and protein, this avocado toast is a satisfying and nutritious breakfast option.

Prep: 10 mins | Cook: 10 mins | Serves: 2 (4 pancakes)

Ingredients:
- 1/2 cup almond flour (US) / 60g almond flour (UK)
- 2 tablespoons coconut flour (US) / 15g coconut flour (UK)
- 2 tablespoons pumpkin puree
- 2 large eggs
- 1/4 cup unsweetened almond milk (US) / 60ml unsweetened almond milk (UK)
- 1 tablespoon granulated sweetener (optional)
- 1 teaspoon baking powder
- 1/2 teaspoon pumpkin pie spice
- 1/4 teaspoon vanilla extract
- Butter or oil for cooking

Instructions:
1. In a mixing bowl, whisk together almond flour, coconut flour, baking powder, pumpkin pie spice, and granulated sweetener (if using).
2. In another bowl, whisk together eggs, pumpkin puree, almond milk, and vanilla extract until smooth.
3. Pour the wet ingredients into the dry ingredients and mix until well combined and smooth.
4. Heat a nonstick skillet or griddle over medium heat and lightly grease with butter or oil.
5. Pour 1/4 cup of the pancake batter onto the skillet for each pancake.
6. Cook for 23 minutes on each side, or until golden brown and cooked through.
7. Serve the pumpkin pancakes warm with your favorite lowcarb syrup or toppings.

Nutritional Info (per serving 2 pancakes): Calories: 250 | Fat: 18g | Carbs: 10g | Protein: 10g

Atkins Diet Feature: Low in carbs and glutenfree, these pumpkin pancakes are a delicious fallinspired breakfast option.

Blueberry Coconut Pancakes

Prep: 10 mins | Cook: 10 mins | Serves: 2 (4 pancakes)

Ingredients:
- 1/2 cup almond flour (US) / 60g almond flour (UK)
- 2 tablespoons coconut flour (US) / 15g coconut flour (UK)
- 2 large eggs
- 1/4 cup unsweetened almond milk (US) / 60ml unsweetened almond milk (UK)
- 1/2 teaspoon baking powder
- 1/4 teaspoon vanilla extract
- 1/4 cup fresh blueberries
- Butter or oil for cooking

Instructions:
1. In a mixing bowl, whisk together almond flour, coconut flour, and baking powder.
2. In another bowl, whisk together eggs, almond milk, and vanilla extract until smooth.
3. Pour the wet ingredients into the dry ingredients and mix until well combined.
4. Gently fold in the fresh blueberries.
5. Heat a nonstick skillet or griddle over medium heat and lightly grease with butter or oil.
6. Pour 1/4 cup of the pancake batter onto the skillet for each pancake.
7. Cook for 23 minutes on each side, or until golden brown and cooked through.
8. Serve the blueberry coconut pancakes warm with a drizzle of sugarfree syrup if desired.

Nutritional Info (per serving 2 pancakes): Calories: 280 | Fat: 20g | Carbs: 10g | Protein: 12g

Atkins Diet Feature: Low in carbs and packed with protein, these blueberry coconut pancakes are a tasty twist on a classic breakfast favorite.

Sausage and Egg Muffin Cups

Prep: 10 mins | Cook: 20 mins | Serves: 4 muffin cups

Ingredients:
- 4 cooked breakfast sausage patties
- 4 large eggs
- Salt and pepper to taste
- Chopped chives for garnish (optional)

Instructions:
1. Preheat your oven to 375°F (190°C). Grease four cups of a muffin tin.
2. Place a cooked sausage patty in each greased muffin cup.
3. Crack an egg into each muffin cup on top of the sausage.
4. Season each egg with salt and pepper.
5. Bake in the preheated oven for 1520 minutes or until the egg whites are set.
6. Remove from the oven and let cool for a few minutes before removing from the muffin tin.
7. Garnish with chopped chives if desired and serve warm.
8. These sausage and egg muffin cups are a convenient and proteinpacked breakfast option.

Nutritional Info (per muffin cup): Calories: 220 | Fat: 16g | Carbs: 1g | Protein: 18g

Atkins Diet Feature: Low in carbs and high in protein, these muffin cups are perfect for meal prep or a quick breakfast on busy mornings.

Egg Bake with Peppers and Onions

Prep: 15 mins | Cook: 30 mins | Serves: 4

Ingredients:

- 6 large eggs
- 1/4 cup heavy cream (US) / 60ml heavy cream (UK)
- 1/2 cup diced bell peppers (US) / 75g diced bell peppers (UK)
- 1/2 cup diced onions (US) / 75g diced onions (UK)
- 1/2 cup shredded cheddar cheese (US) / 50g shredded cheddar cheese (UK)
- Salt and pepper to taste

Instructions:

1. Preheat your oven to 375°F (190°C). Grease a baking dish.
2. In a mixing bowl, whisk together eggs, heavy cream, salt, and pepper.
3. Stir in diced bell peppers, diced onions, and shredded cheddar cheese.
4. Pour the mixture into the prepared baking dish.
5. Bake for 2530 minutes or until the egg bake is set and the top is lightly golden.
6. Allow the egg bake to cool for a few minutes before slicing and serving.
7. This egg bake with peppers and onions is a flavorful and satisfying breakfast option for the Atkins Diet.

Nutritional Info (per serving): Calories: 270 | Fat: 20g | Carbs: 4g | Protein: 18g

Atkins Diet Feature: High in protein and low in carbs, this egg bake is a great way to start your day on the Atkins Diet.

Prep: 15 mins | Cook: 20 mins | Serves: 6 cups

Ingredients:
- 6 large eggs
- 1/4 cup heavy cream (US) / 60ml heavy cream (UK)
- 1/2 cup cooked and crumbled breakfast sausage (US) / 75g cooked and crumbled breakfast sausage (UK)
- 1/4 cup diced bell peppers (US) / 40g diced bell peppers (UK)
- 1/4 cup diced onions (US) / 40g diced onions (UK)
- 1/2 cup shredded cheddar cheese (US) / 50g shredded cheddar cheese (UK)
- Salt and pepper to taste
- 6 lowcarb tortillas, cut into quarters

Instructions:
1. Preheat your oven to 375°F (190°C). Lightly grease a muffin tin.
2. In a mixing bowl, whisk together eggs, heavy cream, salt, and pepper until well combined.
3. Stir in cooked breakfast sausage, diced bell peppers, diced onions, and shredded cheddar cheese.
4. Place a quarter of a lowcarb tortilla into each muffin cup, pressing down gently to form a cup shape.
5. Pour the egg mixture evenly into each tortilla cup, filling almost to the top.
6. Bake in the preheated oven for 1520 minutes or until the eggs are set and the edges of the tortillas are golden brown.
7. Remove from the oven and let cool for a few minutes before carefully removing the breakfast burrito cups from the muffin tin.
8. Serve warm and enjoy these delicious breakfast burrito cups!

Nutritional Info (per cup): Calories: 220 | Fat: 15g | Carbs: 8g | Protein: 15g

Atkins Diet Feature: These breakfast burrito cups are a convenient and portable way to enjoy a lowcarb breakfast, perfect for meal prep or busy mornings on the Atkins Diet.

CHAPTER TWO: APPETIZERS AND SNACKS

Avocado Deviled Eggs

Prep: 15 mins | Cook: 10 mins | Serves: 6

Ingredients:
- 6 large eggs
- 1 ripe avocado
- 2 tablespoons mayonnaise
- 1 teaspoon Dijon mustard
- 1 tablespoon lemon juice
- Salt and pepper to taste
- Paprika for garnish

Instructions:
1. Place eggs in a pot and cover with water. Bring to a boil, then reduce heat and simmer for 10 minutes.
2. Transfer eggs to an ice bath and let cool. Once cool, peel the eggs and cut them in half lengthwise. Remove the yolks and place them in a bowl.
3. Add the avocado, mayonnaise, Dijon mustard, lemon juice, salt, and pepper to the bowl with the egg yolks.
4. Mash everything together until smooth and creamy.
5. Spoon or pipe the avocado mixture into the egg white halves.
6. Sprinkle with paprika for garnish.
7. Serve chilled and enjoy these creamy avocado deviled eggs!

Nutritional Info (per serving 2 halves): Calories: 140 | Fat: 11g | Carbs: 3g | Protein: 7g

Atkins Diet Feature: Rich in healthy fats and protein, these avocado deviled eggs are a satisfying and lowcarb appetizer option.

Prep: 20 mins | Cook: 20 mins | Serves: 4

Ingredients:
- 8 large jalapeno peppers
- 8 slices bacon
- 4 oz cream cheese, softened
- 1/4 cup shredded cheddar cheese
- 1/2 teaspoon garlic powder
- Toothpicks

Instructions:
1. Preheat your oven to 400°F (200°C). Line a baking sheet with parchment paper.
2. Slice the jalapeno peppers in half lengthwise and remove the seeds and membranes.
3. In a bowl, mix together the cream cheese, shredded cheddar cheese, and garlic powder until well combined.
4. Fill each jalapeno half with the cheese mixture.
5. Wrap each stuffed jalapeno with a slice of bacon and secure with a toothpick.
6. Place the baconwrapped jalapeno poppers on the prepared baking sheet.
7. Bake in the preheated oven for 20 minutes or until the bacon is crispy and the peppers are tender.
8. Allow to cool for a few minutes before serving.
9. Enjoy these delicious jalapeno poppers as a spicy and savory snack!

Nutritional Info (per serving 2 poppers): Calories: 240 | Fat: 20g | Carbs: 3g | Protein: 10g

Atkins Diet Feature: These jalapeno poppers are low in carbs and high in fat, making them a perfect snack for the Atkins Diet.

Prep: 10 mins | Cook: 20 mins | Serves: 6

Ingredients:
- 1 can (15 oz) chickpeas, drained and rinsed
- 1/4 cup roasted red peppers, drained
- 2 tablespoons tahini
- 2 cloves garlic, minced
- 2 tablespoons lemon juice
- 2 tablespoons olive oil
- Salt and pepper to taste
- Paprika for garnish (optional)

Instructions:
1. Preheat your oven to 400°F (200°C).
2. Place the drained chickpeas on a baking sheet lined with parchment paper. Roast in the preheated oven for 1520 minutes until slightly crispy.
3. In a food processor, combine the roasted chickpeas, roasted red peppers, tahini, minced garlic, lemon juice, olive oil, salt, and pepper.
4. Blend until smooth and creamy, scraping down the sides as needed.
5. If the hummus is too thick, you can add a little water to achieve your desired consistency.
6. Taste and adjust seasoning if necessary.
7. Transfer the hummus to a serving bowl, sprinkle with paprika for garnish if desired.
8. Serve with your favorite lowcarb vegetables or crackers.
9. Enjoy this flavorful roasted red pepper hummus as a delicious and healthy snack!

Nutritional Info (per serving 1/4 cup): Calories: 150 | Fat: 9g | Carbs: 14g | Protein: 4g

Atkins Diet Feature: This roasted red pepper hummus is lower in carbs compared to traditional hummus and provides a good source of protein and healthy fats, making it suitable for the Atkins Diet.

Prep: 15 mins | Cook: 20 mins | Serves: 4

Ingredients:
- 12 large mushrooms
- 6 slices bacon, halved
- 4 oz cream cheese, softened
- 1/4 cup grated Parmesan cheese
- 2 cloves garlic, minced
- 1 tablespoon chopped fresh parsley
- Salt and pepper to taste

Instructions:
1. Preheat your oven to 375°F (190°C). Line a baking sheet with parchment paper.
2. Clean the mushrooms and remove the stems. Set aside.
3. In a bowl, mix together the cream cheese, Parmesan cheese, minced garlic, chopped parsley, salt, and pepper until well combined.
4. Stuff each mushroom cap with the cream cheese mixture.
5. Wrap each stuffed mushroom with half a slice of bacon and secure with a toothpick.
6. Place the baconwrapped mushrooms on the prepared baking sheet.
7. Bake in the preheated oven for 20 minutes or until the bacon is crispy and the mushrooms are tender.
8. Allow to cool for a few minutes before serving.
9. Enjoy these savory baconwrapped stuffed mushrooms as a tasty appetizer or snack!

Nutritional Info (per serving 3 mushrooms): Calories: 220 | Fat: 18g | Carbs: 4g | Protein: 10g

Atkins Diet Feature: These baconwrapped stuffed mushrooms are low in carbs and high in fat and protein, making them a delicious and satisfying option for the Atkins Diet.

Prep: 10 mins | Cook: 10 mins | Serves: 4

Ingredients:
- 1 bunch asparagus spears, tough ends trimmed
- 8 slices prosciutto
- 1 tablespoon olive oil
- Salt and pepper to taste
- Lemon wedges for serving (optional)

Instructions:
1. Preheat your oven to 400°F (200°C).
2. Toss the asparagus spears with olive oil, salt, and pepper until evenly coated.
3. Divide the asparagus spears into bundles of 34 spears each.
4. Wrap each asparagus bundle with a slice of prosciutto.
5. Place the prosciuttowrapped asparagus bundles on a baking sheet lined with parchment paper.
6. Bake in the preheated oven for 810 minutes or until the asparagus is tender and the prosciutto is crispy.
7. Remove from the oven and let cool for a few minutes before serving.
8. Serve with lemon wedges if desired.
9. Enjoy these elegant prosciuttowrapped asparagus spears as a delicious and lowcarb appetizer!

Nutritional Info (per serving 4 asparagus bundles): Calories: 160 | Fat: 9g | Carbs: 4g | Protein: 10g

Atkins Diet Feature: Low in carbs and rich in protein and healthy fats, these prosciuttowrapped asparagus bundles are a flavorful and satisfying snack option for the Atkins Diet.

Meat and Cheese RollUps

Prep: 10 mins | Cook: 0 mins | Serves: 4

Ingredients:
- 8 slices deli meat (such as turkey, ham, or roast beef)
- 4 slices cheese (such as cheddar, Swiss, or provolone)
- Mustard or mayo (optional)
- Toothpicks

Instructions:
1. Lay out a slice of deli meat on a clean surface.
2. Place a slice of cheese on top of the meat.
3. Add a thin layer of mustard or mayo on top of the cheese, if desired.
4. Roll up the meat and cheese tightly.
5. Secure with a toothpick.
6. Repeat with the remaining slices of deli meat and cheese.
7. Serve the meat and cheese rollups as a quick and easy lowcarb snack or appetizer.
8. Enjoy these tasty rollups as a satisfying proteinpacked snack on the Atkins Diet!

Nutritional Info (per serving 2 rollups): Calories: 180 | Fat: 12g | Carbs: 1g | Protein: 16g

Atkins Diet Feature: High in protein and low in carbs, these meat and cheese rollups are a convenient and delicious snack option for the Atkins Diet.

Prep: 15 mins | Cook: 0 mins | Serves: 4

Ingredients:
- 1 large cucumber
- 4 oz cream cheese, softened
- 1 tablespoon chopped fresh dill
- 1 teaspoon lemon juice
- Salt and pepper to taste
- Cherry tomatoes or olives for garnish (optional)

Instructions:
1. Wash the cucumber and slice it into rounds, about 1/2 inch thick.
2. In a bowl, mix together the softened cream cheese, chopped fresh dill, lemon juice, salt, and pepper until well combined.
3. Spread a small amount of the cream cheese mixture onto each cucumber round.
4. Garnish with cherry tomatoes or olives if desired.
5. Serve the cucumber bites chilled and enjoy this refreshing and lowcarb snack option!
6. These cucumber bites with cream cheese are a light and satisfying snack choice for the Atkins Diet.

Nutritional Info (per serving 4 cucumber bites): Calories: 90 | Fat: 8g | Carbs: 3g | Protein: 2g

Atkins Diet Feature: Low in carbs and rich in flavor, these cucumber bites with cream cheese are a perfect snack to enjoy while following the Atkins Diet.

Prep: 15 mins | Cook: 20 mins | Serves: 4

Ingredients:
- 2 large zucchinis
- 1/2 cup almond flour
- 1/4 cup grated Parmesan cheese
- 1 teaspoon garlic powder
- 1 teaspoon paprika
- 2 large eggs, beaten
- Salt and pepper to taste
- Cooking spray

Instructions:
1. Preheat your oven to 425°F (220°C). Line a baking sheet with parchment paper and lightly coat with cooking spray.
2. Cut the zucchinis into fryshaped sticks.
3. In a shallow dish, mix together the almond flour, grated Parmesan cheese, garlic powder, paprika, salt, and pepper.
4. Dip each zucchini stick into the beaten eggs, then coat with the almond flour mixture, pressing gently to adhere.
5. Place the coated zucchini fries in a single layer on the prepared baking sheet.
6. Bake in the preheated oven for 2025 minutes, flipping halfway through, until the fries are golden brown and crispy.
7. Remove from the oven and let cool for a few minutes before serving.
8. Enjoy these crispy zucchini fries with your favorite lowcarb dipping sauce!

Nutritional Info (per serving): Calories: 120 | Fat: 7g | Carbs: 6g | Protein: 8g

Atkins Diet Feature: These zucchini fries are a tasty and crunchy alternative to traditional potato fries, perfect for those following the Atkins Diet.

Prep: 15 mins | Cook: 25 mins | Serves: 4

Ingredients:
For the Meatballs:

- 1 lb ground beef
- 1/4 cup almond flour
- 1/4 cup grated Parmesan cheese
- 1 egg
- 2 cloves garlic, minced
- 1 teaspoon Italian seasoning
- Salt and pepper to taste

For the Tomato Sauce:

- 1 can (14 oz) crushed tomatoes
- 2 cloves garlic, minced
- 1 teaspoon Italian seasoning
- Salt and pepper to taste
- Fresh basil leaves for garnish (optional)

Instructions:
1. Preheat your oven to 375°F (190°C). Line a baking sheet with parchment paper.
2. In a large bowl, combine the ground beef, almond flour, grated Parmesan cheese, egg, minced garlic, Italian seasoning, salt, and pepper. Mix until well combined.
3. Shape the mixture into meatballs, about 1 inch in diameter, and place them on the prepared baking sheet.
4. Bake in the preheated oven for 2025 minutes, or until the meatballs are cooked through and browned on the outside.
5. While the meatballs are baking, prepare the tomato sauce. In a saucepan, combine the crushed tomatoes, minced garlic, Italian seasoning, salt, and pepper. Bring to a simmer and cook for 510 minutes, until the sauce has thickened slightly.
6. Once the meatballs are cooked, transfer them to the saucepan with the tomato sauce. Gently stir to coat the meatballs in the sauce.
7. Serve the meatballs with tomato sauce hot, garnished with fresh basil leaves if desired.

8. Enjoy these flavorful meatballs with tomato sauce as a hearty and satisfying Atkins Dietfriendly snack or appetizer!

Nutritional Info (per serving): Calories: 320 | Fat: 20g | Carbs: 8g | Protein: 25g

Atkins Diet Feature: These meatballs are made with almond flour instead of breadcrumbs, making them low in carbs and suitable for the Atkins Diet. Plus, they're packed with protein and flavor!

Caprese Salad Skewers

Prep: 15 mins | Cook: 0 mins | Serves: 4

Ingredients:
- 1 pint cherry tomatoes
- 8 oz fresh mozzarella cheese, cut into cubes
- Fresh basil leaves
- Balsamic glaze for drizzling
- Wooden skewers

Instructions:
1. Thread a cherry tomato, a cube of fresh mozzarella cheese, and a fresh basil leaf onto each wooden skewer.
2. Repeat until all ingredients are used, making about 12 skewers.
3. Arrange the skewers on a serving platter.
4. Drizzle the skewers with balsamic glaze just before serving.
5. Enjoy these vibrant and flavorful caprese salad skewers as a refreshing and lowcarb appetizer or snack option on the Atkins Diet!

Nutritional Info (per serving 3 skewers): Calories: 180 | Fat: 12g | Carbs: 6g | Protein: 12g

Atkins Diet Feature: These caprese salad skewers are light, refreshing, and low in carbs, making them a perfect choice for the Atkins Diet. Plus, they're a breeze to put together and look impressive on any appetizer spread!

Cauliflower Buffalo Bites

Prep: 15 mins | Cook: 20 mins | Serves: 4

Ingredients:
- 1 head cauliflower, cut into florets
- 1/2 cup almond flour
- 1/2 teaspoon garlic powder
- 1/2 teaspoon paprika
- Salt and pepper to taste
- 1/4 cup hot sauce
- 2 tablespoons melted butter
- Ranch or blue cheese dressing for dipping (optional)

Instructions:
1. Preheat your oven to 450°F (230°C). Line a baking sheet with parchment paper.
2. In a large bowl, combine the almond flour, garlic powder, paprika, salt, and pepper.
3. Toss the cauliflower florets in the almond flour mixture until evenly coated.
4. Arrange the coated cauliflower florets in a single layer on the prepared baking sheet.
5. Bake in the preheated oven for 1520 minutes, or until the cauliflower is golden brown and crispy.
6. In a separate bowl, mix together the hot sauce and melted butter.
7. Remove the cauliflower from the oven and drizzle with the hot sauce mixture, tossing to coat evenly.
8. Return the cauliflower to the oven and bake for an additional 5 minutes.
9. Serve the cauliflower buffalo bites hot, with ranch or blue cheese dressing for dipping if desired.
10. Enjoy these spicy and flavorful cauliflower buffalo bites as a satisfying and lowcarb snack or appetizer on the Atkins Diet!

Nutritional Info (per serving): Calories: 150 | Fat: 10g | Carbs: 8g | Protein: 6g

Atkins Diet Feature: These cauliflower buffalo bites are a delicious and lowcarb alternative to traditional buffalo wings, perfect for satisfying cravings while following the Atkins Diet.

Tuna Salad Stuffed Celery

Prep: 10 mins | Cook: 0 mins | Serves: 4

Ingredients:
- 4 stalks celery
- 1 can (5 oz) tuna, drained
- 2 tablespoons mayonnaise
- 1 tablespoon chopped fresh parsley
- 1 tablespoon lemon juice
- Salt and pepper to taste
- Paprika for garnish (optional)

Instructions:
1. Wash the celery stalks and trim off the ends.
2. In a bowl, mix together the drained tuna, mayonnaise, chopped fresh parsley, lemon juice, salt, and pepper until well combined.
3. Fill each celery stalk with the tuna salad mixture.
4. Sprinkle with paprika for garnish if desired.
5. Serve the tuna salad stuffed celery stalks chilled and enjoy this light and refreshing snack option!
6. These tuna salad stuffed celery stalks are low in carbs and high in protein, making them a perfect snack for the Atkins Diet.

Nutritional Info (per serving 1 celery stalk): Calories: 80 | Fat: 5g | Carbs: 2g | Protein: 8g

Atkins Diet Feature: This tuna salad stuffed celery is a convenient and satisfying snack option that's low in carbs and rich in protein, perfect for the Atkins Diet.

Greek Yogurt Ranch Dip

Prep: 5 mins | Cook: 0 mins | Serves: 6

Ingredients:
- 1 cup Greek yogurt
- 1 tablespoon chopped fresh dill
- 1 tablespoon chopped fresh chives
- 1 teaspoon onion powder
- 1 teaspoon garlic powder
- Salt and pepper to taste

Instructions:
1. In a bowl, combine the Greek yogurt, chopped fresh dill, chopped fresh chives, onion powder, garlic powder, salt, and pepper.
2. Mix until well combined.
3. Taste and adjust seasoning if necessary.
4. Serve the Greek yogurt ranch dip with your favorite lowcarb vegetables or chips.
5. Enjoy this creamy and flavorful dip as a delicious and guiltfree snack option on the Atkins Diet!

Nutritional Info (per serving 2 tablespoons): Calories: 40 | Fat: 0g | Carbs: 3g | Protein: 6g

Atkins Diet Feature: This Greek yogurt ranch dip is made with proteinrich Greek yogurt and flavored with fresh herbs, making it a healthy and lowcarb option for dipping veggies or chips on the Atkins Diet.

Cheesy Broccoli Tots

Prep: 20 mins | Cook: 20 mins | Serves: 4

Ingredients:
- 2 cups chopped broccoli florets
- 1/2 cup shredded cheddar cheese
- 1/4 cup almond flour
- 1 egg
- 1/4 teaspoon garlic powder
- Salt and pepper to taste
- Cooking spray

Instructions:
1. Preheat your oven to 400°F (200°C). Line a baking sheet with parchment paper and lightly coat with cooking spray.
2. Steam the chopped broccoli florets until tender, then let them cool slightly.
3. In a large bowl, combine the steamed broccoli, shredded cheddar cheese, almond flour, egg, garlic powder, salt, and pepper. Mix until well combined.
4. Shape the mixture into tots, about 1 inch in size, and place them on the prepared baking sheet.
5. Bake in the preheated oven for 1820 minutes, flipping halfway through, until the tots are golden brown and crispy.
6. Remove from the oven and let cool for a few minutes before serving.
7. Enjoy these cheesy broccoli tots as a delicious and nutritious snack or side dish on the Atkins Diet!

Nutritional Info (per serving): Calories: 120 | Fat: 8g | Carbs: 5g | Protein: 7g

Atkins Diet Feature: These cheesy broccoli tots are low in carbs and packed with flavor, making them a satisfying and wholesome snack option for the Atkins Diet.

CHAPTER THREE: SALADS AND DRESSINGS

Crispy Chicken Caesar Salad

Prep: 15 mins | Cook: 15 mins | Serves: 4

Ingredients:
- 2 boneless, skinless chicken breasts (about 8 oz each) (450g)
- 1 tablespoon olive oil (15ml)
- Salt and pepper to taste
- 1 head romaine lettuce, chopped (1 head)
- 1/2 cup grated Parmesan cheese (50g)
- 1 cup croutons (100g)
- Caesar dressing (storebought or homemade)
- Lemon wedges for garnish (optional)

Instructions:
1. Preheat your grill or skillet over mediumhigh heat.
2. Rub the chicken breasts with olive oil and season with salt and pepper.
3. Grill or cook the chicken breasts for about 68 minutes on each side, or until cooked through and no longer pink in the center.
4. Remove the chicken from the grill or skillet and let it rest for a few minutes. Then, slice it thinly.
5. In a large bowl, toss together the chopped romaine lettuce, grated Parmesan cheese, and croutons.
6. Add the sliced chicken to the salad.
7. Drizzle with Caesar dressing and toss to coat evenly.
8. Divide the salad among serving plates.
9. Garnish with lemon wedges if desired.
10. Serve immediately and enjoy this delicious and satisfying crispy chicken Caesar salad!

Nutritional Info (per serving): Calories: 320 | Fat: 15g | Carbs: 15g | Protein: 30g

Atkins Diet Feature: This chicken Caesar salad is high in protein and low in carbs, making it a perfect meal option for the Atkins Diet. Plus, it's packed with flavor and crunch!

TexMex Taco Salad

Prep: 20 mins | Cook: 10 mins | Serves: 4

Ingredients:
- 1 lb ground beef (450g)
- 1 packet taco seasoning mix
- 1 head iceberg lettuce, shredded (1 head)
- 1 cup shredded cheddar cheese (100g)
- 1 cup cherry tomatoes, halved (150g)
- 1/2 cup sliced black olives (50g)
- 1/4 cup chopped fresh cilantro (15g)
- 1/2 cup sour cream (120ml)
- 1/4 cup salsa (60ml)
- Lime wedges for garnish (optional)

Instructions:
1. In a skillet, cook the ground beef over medium heat until browned and cooked through.
2. Drain excess fat from the skillet, then add the taco seasoning mix and cook according to package instructions.
3. In a large bowl, combine the shredded iceberg lettuce, shredded cheddar cheese, cherry tomatoes, sliced black olives, and chopped fresh cilantro.
4. Add the cooked taco meat to the salad and toss to combine.
5. In a small bowl, mix together the sour cream and salsa to make the dressing.
6. Drizzle the dressing over the salad and toss to coat evenly.
7. Divide the salad among serving plates.
8. Garnish with lime wedges if desired.
9. Serve immediately and enjoy this flavorful TexMex taco salad!

Nutritional Info (per serving): Calories: 420 | Fat: 30g | Carbs: 10g | Protein: 25g

Atkins Diet Feature: This TexMex taco salad is low in carbs and high in protein, making it a satisfying and delicious option for the Atkins Diet. Plus, it's loaded with vibrant flavors and textures!

Prep: 20 mins | Cook: 10 mins | Serves: 4

Ingredients:
- 2 boneless, skinless chicken breasts (about 8 oz each) (450g)
- 1 tablespoon olive oil (15ml)
- Salt and pepper to taste
- 1 head romaine lettuce, chopped (1 head)
- 1 cup cherry tomatoes, halved (150g)
- 1 cucumber, diced (1 cucumber)
- 1/2 red onion, thinly sliced (1/2 onion)
- 1/2 cup Kalamata olives (50g)
- 1/2 cup crumbled feta cheese (50g)
- Greek salad dressing (storebought or homemade)
- Lemon wedges for garnish (optional)

Instructions:
1. Preheat your grill or skillet over mediumhigh heat.
2. Rub the chicken breasts with olive oil and season with salt and pepper.
3. Grill or cook the chicken breasts for about 68 minutes on each side, or until cooked through and no longer pink in the center.
4. Remove the chicken from the grill or skillet and let it rest for a few minutes. Then, slice it thinly.
5. In a large bowl, combine the chopped romaine lettuce, cherry tomatoes, diced cucumber, thinly sliced red onion, Kalamata olives, and crumbled feta cheese.
6. Add the sliced chicken to the salad.
7. Drizzle with Greek salad dressing and toss to coat evenly.
8. Divide the salad among serving plates.
9. Garnish with lemon wedges if desired.
10. Serve immediately and enjoy this refreshing and flavorful Greek salad with grilled chicken!

Nutritional Info (per serving): Calories: 350 | Fat: 20g | Carbs: 10g | Protein: 30g

Atkins Diet Feature: This Greek salad with grilled chicken is a nutritious and satisfying meal option for the Atkins Diet. It's packed with protein, healthy fats, and fresh vegetables, making it a perfect choice for a lowcarb lifestyle!

Prep: 15 mins | Cook: 10 mins | Serves: 4

Ingredients:
- 6 cups mixed salad greens (360g)
- 8 slices deli turkey or ham, chopped (200g)
- 4 hardboiled eggs, sliced (4 eggs)
- 1 cup cherry tomatoes, halved (150g)
- 1/2 cucumber, sliced (1/2 cucumber)
- 1/2 cup shredded cheddar cheese (50g)
- 1/4 cup sliced red onion (1/4 onion)
- 1/4 cup sliced black olives (25g)
- Your favorite lowcarb salad dressing

Instructions:
1. In a large bowl, combine the mixed salad greens, chopped deli turkey or ham, sliced hardboiled eggs, cherry tomatoes, sliced cucumber, shredded cheddar cheese, sliced red onion, and sliced black olives.
2. Toss the salad ingredients together until evenly distributed.
3. Divide the salad among serving plates.
4. Serve with your favorite lowcarb salad dressing on the side.
5. Enjoy this classic chef salad with hardboiled eggs and deli meat as a satisfying and nutritious meal option on the Atkins Diet!

Nutritional Info (per serving): Calories: 320 | Fat: 20g | Carbs: 8g | Protein: 25g

Atkins Diet Feature: This classic chef salad is low in carbs and high in protein, making it an excellent choice for the Atkins Diet. Packed with fresh vegetables, deli meat, and hardboiled eggs, it's a balanced and satisfying meal!

Refreshing Spinach Salad with Strawberries, Almonds, and Feta

Prep: 15 mins | Cook: 0 mins | Serves: 4

Ingredients:
- 6 cups fresh baby spinach (360g)
- 1 cup sliced strawberries (150g)
- 1/2 cup sliced almonds (50g)
- 1/4 cup crumbled feta cheese (50g)
- Balsamic vinaigrette dressing

Instructions:
1. In a large bowl, combine the fresh baby spinach, sliced strawberries, sliced almonds, and crumbled feta cheese.
2. Toss the salad ingredients together until evenly distributed.
3. Divide the salad among serving plates.
4. Drizzle with balsamic vinaigrette dressing just before serving.
5. Enjoy this refreshing spinach salad with strawberries, almonds, and feta as a light and flavorful meal option on the Atkins Diet!

Nutritional Info (per serving): Calories: 180 | Fat: 12g | Carbs: 10g | Protein: 8g

Atkins Diet Feature: This spinach salad is low in carbs and packed with nutrients, making it a perfect choice for the Atkins Diet. The combination of sweet strawberries, crunchy almonds, and tangy feta cheese creates a delicious flavor profile!

Classic Cobb Salad

Prep: 20 mins | Cook: 10 mins | Serves: 4

Ingredients:
- 6 cups mixed salad greens (360g)
- 2 boneless, skinless chicken breasts, grilled and diced (8 oz each, 450g)
- 8 slices cooked bacon, crumbled (200g)
- 4 hardboiled eggs, chopped (4 eggs)
- 1 avocado, diced (1 avocado)
- 1 cup cherry tomatoes, halved (150g)
- 1/2 cup crumbled blue cheese (50g)
- Your favorite lowcarb salad dressing

Instructions:
1. In a large bowl, combine the mixed salad greens, grilled and diced chicken breasts, crumbled bacon, chopped hardboiled eggs, diced avocado, cherry tomatoes, and crumbled blue cheese.
2. Toss the salad ingredients together until evenly distributed.
3. Divide the salad among serving plates.
4. Serve with your favorite lowcarb salad dressing on the side.
5. Enjoy this classic Cobb salad as a hearty and satisfying meal option on the Atkins Diet!

Nutritional Info (per serving): Calories: 420 | Fat: 30g | Carbs: 10g | Protein: 25g

Atkins Diet Feature: This classic Cobb salad is rich in protein and healthy fats, making it a filling and nutritious meal choice for the Atkins Diet. With a variety of textures and flavors, it's sure to satisfy your cravings!

Bacon Ranch Chopped Salad

Prep: 20 mins | Cook: 10 mins | Serves: 4

Ingredients:
- 6 cups mixed salad greens (360g)
- 8 slices cooked bacon, crumbled (200g)
- 1 cup cherry tomatoes, halved (150g)
- 1/2 cup shredded cheddar cheese (50g)
- 1/4 cup chopped green onions (15g)
- Ranch dressing (storebought or homemade)

Instructions:
1. In a large bowl, combine the mixed salad greens, crumbled bacon, cherry tomatoes, shredded cheddar cheese, and chopped green onions.
2. Toss the salad ingredients together until evenly distributed.
3. Divide the salad among serving plates.
4. Drizzle with ranch dressing just before serving.
5. Enjoy this flavorful bacon ranch chopped salad as a delicious and satisfying meal option on the Atkins Diet!

Nutritional Info (per serving): Calories: 320 | Fat: 25g | Carbs: 10g | Protein: 15g

Atkins Diet Feature: This bacon ranch chopped salad is low in carbs and packed with protein and flavor, making it an ideal choice for the Atkins Diet. The combination of crispy bacon, sharp cheddar cheese, and creamy ranch dressing is irresistible!

Chicken Bacon Ranch Salad

Prep: 20 mins | Cook: 15 mins | Serves: 4

Ingredients:
- 2 boneless, skinless chicken breasts, grilled and sliced (8 oz each, 450g)
- 8 slices cooked bacon, crumbled (200g)
- 6 cups mixed salad greens (360g)
- 1 cup cherry tomatoes, halved (150g)
- 1/2 cup shredded mozzarella cheese (50g)
- Ranch dressing (storebought or homemade)

Instructions:
1. In a large bowl, combine the mixed salad greens, grilled and sliced chicken breasts, crumbled bacon, cherry tomatoes, and shredded mozzarella cheese.
2. Toss the salad ingredients together until evenly distributed.
3. Divide the salad among serving plates.
4. Drizzle with ranch dressing just before serving.
5. Enjoy this delicious chicken bacon ranch salad as a satisfying and proteinpacked meal option on the Atkins Diet!

Nutritional Info (per serving): Calories: 380 | Fat: 25g | Carbs: 10g | Protein: 30g

Atkins Diet Feature: This chicken bacon ranch salad is high in protein and low in carbs, making it a perfect choice for the Atkins Diet. The combination of tender chicken, crispy bacon, and creamy ranch dressing is sure to please your taste buds!

Prep: 15 mins | Cook: 10 mins | Serves: 4

Ingredients:
- 6 cups mixed salad greens (360g)
- 8 slices cooked bacon, crumbled (200g)
- 1 cup cherry tomatoes, halved (150g)
- 1/2 cup croutons (50g)
- Creamy dressing (mayonnaisebased or sour creambased)

Instructions:
1. In a large bowl, combine the mixed salad greens, crumbled bacon, cherry tomatoes, and croutons.
2. Toss the salad ingredients together until evenly distributed.
3. Divide the salad among serving plates.
4. Drizzle with creamy dressing just before serving.
5. Enjoy this BLT salad with creamy dressing as a classic and satisfying meal option on the Atkins Diet!

Nutritional Info (per serving): Calories: 320 | Fat: 25g | Carbs: 10g | Protein: 15g

Atkins Diet Feature: This BLT salad with creamy dressing is low in carbs and packed with flavor, making it a great choice for the Atkins Diet. The combination of crispy bacon, juicy tomatoes, and creamy dressing is simply irresistible!

Prep: 15 mins | Cook: 10 mins | Serves: 4

Ingredients:
- 2 boneless, skinless chicken breasts, cooked and shredded (8 oz each, 450g)
- 2 ripe avocados, diced (2 avocados)
- 1/4 cup diced red onion (1/4 onion)
- 1/4 cup chopped fresh cilantro (15g)
- 1/4 cup mayonnaise (60g)
- 1 tablespoon lime juice (15ml)
- Salt and pepper to taste
- Lettuce leaves for serving

Instructions:
1. In a large bowl, combine the shredded chicken, diced avocado, diced red onion, chopped fresh cilantro, mayonnaise, and lime juice.
2. Season with salt and pepper to taste.
3. Mix until well combined.
4. Serve the avocado chicken salad on lettuce leaves.
5. Enjoy this creamy and flavorful avocado chicken salad as a satisfying and lowcarb meal option on the Atkins Diet!

Nutritional Info (per serving): Calories: 320 | Fat: 25g | Carbs: 10g | Protein: 20g

Atkins Diet Feature: This avocado chicken salad is rich in healthy fats and protein, making it a perfect choice for the Atkins Diet. Plus, it's quick and easy to make, perfect for a busy weeknight meal!

Tuna Salad over Greens

Prep: 10 mins | Cook: 0 mins | Serves: 4

Ingredients:
- 2 cans (5 oz each) tuna, drained (2 cans, 140g each)
- 1/4 cup diced celery (60g)
- 1/4 cup diced red onion (1/4 onion)
- 1/4 cup diced pickles (60g)
- 1/4 cup mayonnaise (60g)
- 1 tablespoon lemon juice (15ml)
- Salt and pepper to taste
- Mixed salad greens for serving

Instructions:
1. In a bowl, combine the drained tuna, diced celery, diced red onion, diced pickles, mayonnaise, and lemon juice.
2. Mix until well combined.
3. Season with salt and pepper to taste.
4. Serve the tuna salad over mixed salad greens.
5. Enjoy this simple and satisfying tuna salad over greens as a nutritious and lowcarb meal option on the Atkins Diet!

Nutritional Info (per serving): Calories: 250 | Fat: 15g | Carbs: 5g | Protein: 20g

Atkins Diet Feature: This tuna salad over greens is high in protein and low in carbs, making it an excellent choice for the Atkins Diet. It's packed with flavor and nutrients, perfect for a quick and easy lunch or dinner!

Egg Salad Lettuce Wraps

Prep: 15 mins | Cook: 10 mins | Serves: 4

Ingredients:
- 6 hardboiled eggs, chopped (6 eggs)
- 1/4 cup mayonnaise (60g)
- 1 tablespoon Dijon mustard (15g)
- 1/4 cup chopped celery (60g)
- 2 tablespoons chopped fresh chives (30g)
- Salt and pepper to taste
- Lettuce leaves for wrapping

Instructions:
1. In a bowl, combine the chopped hardboiled eggs, mayonnaise, Dijon mustard, chopped celery, and chopped fresh chives.
2. Mix until well combined.
3. Season with salt and pepper to taste.
4. Spoon the egg salad onto lettuce leaves.
5. Wrap the lettuce leaves around the egg salad.
6. Serve the egg salad lettuce wraps as a light and flavorful meal option on the Atkins Diet!

Nutritional Info (per serving): Calories: 280 | Fat: 20g | Carbs: 5g | Protein: 15g

Atkins Diet Feature: These egg salad lettuce wraps are low in carbs and high in protein, making them a perfect choice for the Atkins Diet. They're quick to make and incredibly satisfying, ideal for a busy day!

Prep: 15 mins | Cook: 0 mins | Serves: 4

Ingredients:
- 6 cups mixed salad greens (360g)
- 4 oz Genoa salami, thinly sliced (120g)
- 4 oz provolone cheese, thinly sliced (120g)
- 1 cup cherry tomatoes, halved (150g)
- 1/4 cup sliced red onion (1/4 onion)
- 1/4 cup sliced black olives (25g)
- Italian dressing (storebought or homemade)

Instructions:
1. In a large bowl, combine the mixed salad greens, thinly sliced Genoa salami, thinly sliced provolone cheese, cherry tomatoes, sliced red onion, and sliced black olives.
2. Toss the salad ingredients together until evenly distributed.
3. Divide the salad among serving plates.
4. Drizzle with Italian dressing just before serving.
5. Enjoy this flavorful Italian salad with Genoa salami and provolone as a satisfying and delicious meal option on the Atkins Diet!

Nutritional Info (per serving): Calories: 320 | Fat: 25g | Carbs: 10g | Protein: 15g

Atkins Diet Feature: This Italian salad with Genoa salami and provolone is low in carbs and packed with protein and flavor, making it a perfect choice for the Atkins Diet. It's a hearty and satisfying meal that's sure to impress!

Ham Salad with Dijon Vinaigrette

Prep: 15 mins | Cook: 0 mins | Serves: 4

Ingredients:
- 6 cups mixed salad greens (360g)
- 8 oz cooked ham, diced (225g)
- 1/2 cup diced cucumber (1/2 cucumber)
- 1/4 cup diced red bell pepper (1/4 pepper)
- 1/4 cup sliced radishes (50g)
- 1/4 cup crumbled feta cheese (50g)
- Dijon vinaigrette dressing (storebought or homemade)

Instructions:
1. In a large bowl, combine the mixed salad greens, diced cooked ham, diced cucumber, diced red bell pepper, sliced radishes, and crumbled feta cheese.
2. Toss the salad ingredients together until evenly distributed.
3. Divide the salad among serving plates.
4. Drizzle with Dijon vinaigrette dressing just before serving.
5. Enjoy this refreshing ham salad with Dijon vinaigrette as a satisfying and flavorful meal option on the Atkins Diet!

Nutritional Info (per serving): Calories: 280 | Fat: 15g | Carbs: 10g | Protein: 20g

Atkins Diet Feature: This ham salad with Dijon vinaigrette is low in carbs and packed with protein, making it an excellent choice for the Atkins Diet. It's a delicious and nutritious way to enjoy a hearty salad!

Chicken Salad Stuffed Tomatoes

Prep: 15 mins | Cook: 0 mins | Serves: 4

Ingredients:
- 4 large tomatoes
- 2 cups cooked chicken, shredded (300g)
- 1/4 cup diced celery (60g)
- 1/4 cup diced red onion (1/4 onion)
- 1/4 cup diced red bell pepper (1/4 pepper)
- 1/4 cup mayonnaise (60g)
- 1 tablespoon chopped fresh parsley (15g)
- Salt and pepper to taste
- Lettuce leaves for serving

Instructions:
1. Slice the tops off the tomatoes and scoop out the seeds and pulp to create a cavity.
2. In a bowl, combine the shredded cooked chicken, diced celery, diced red onion, diced red bell pepper, mayonnaise, chopped fresh parsley, salt, and pepper.
3. Mix until well combined.
4. Spoon the chicken salad into the hollowedout tomatoes.
5. Serve the chicken salad stuffed tomatoes on lettuce leaves.
6. Enjoy this tasty and creative chicken salad as a satisfying and lowcarb meal option on the Atkins Diet!

Nutritional Info (per serving): Calories: 250 | Fat: 15g | Carbs: 10g | Protein: 20g

Atkins Diet Feature: These chicken salad stuffed tomatoes are low in carbs and high in protein, making them a perfect choice for the Atkins Diet. They're a fun and delicious twist on traditional chicken salad!

CHAPTER FOUR: SOUPS AND STEWS

Creamy Zucchini Soup with Parmesan Crisps

Prep: 10 mins | Cook: 25 mins | Serves: 4

Ingredients:
- 2 medium zucchinis, sliced (about 400g)
- 1 tablespoon olive oil (15ml)
- 1 onion, chopped (1 onion)
- 2 cloves garlic, minced (2 cloves)
- 4 cups vegetable broth (960ml)
- Salt and pepper to taste
- 1/4 cup heavy cream (60ml)
- 1/4 cup grated Parmesan cheese (25g)
- 1 tablespoon chopped fresh parsley for garnish (15g)

Instructions:
1. Heat olive oil in a large pot over medium heat. Add chopped onion and minced garlic. Sauté until softened, about 5 minutes.
2. Add sliced zucchinis to the pot and cook for another 5 minutes, stirring occasionally.
3. Pour in vegetable broth and bring to a simmer. Let it cook for 15 minutes until the zucchinis are tender.
4. Use an immersion blender to blend the soup until smooth. Alternatively, transfer the soup to a blender and blend in batches until smooth.
5. Season with salt and pepper to taste. Stir in heavy cream and let it simmer for another 5 minutes.
6. In a separate nonstick pan, sprinkle grated Parmesan cheese to form thin circles. Cook until the edges are golden and crispy, about 23 minutes per side.
7. Ladle the creamy zucchini soup into serving bowls. Top each serving with a Parmesan crisp and chopped fresh parsley.
8. Serve hot and enjoy this comforting and nutritious creamy zucchini soup!

Nutritional Info (per serving): Calories: 180 | Fat: 12g | Carbs: 8g | Protein: 5g

Atkins Diet Feature: This creamy zucchini soup is low in carbs and high in fiber, making it suitable for the Atkins Diet. The addition of heavy cream and Parmesan cheese provides richness without compromising on flavor!

Rich and Velvety Broccoli Cheese Soup

Prep: 15 mins | Cook: 25 mins | Serves: 4

Ingredients:
- 2 cups broccoli florets (about 250g)
- 1 tablespoon butter (15g)
- 1 onion, chopped (1 onion)
- 2 cloves garlic, minced (2 cloves)
- 4 cups chicken or vegetable broth (960ml)
- Salt and pepper to taste
- 1 cup shredded cheddar cheese (100g)
- 1/2 cup heavy cream (120ml)
- Crispy bacon bits for garnish (optional)

Instructions:
1. In a large pot, melt butter over medium heat. Add chopped onion and minced garlic. Sauté until fragrant and softened, about 5 minutes.
2. Add broccoli florets to the pot and pour in chicken or vegetable broth. Season with salt and pepper to taste.
3. Bring the mixture to a boil, then reduce the heat and let it simmer for 1520 minutes until the broccoli is tender.
4. Use an immersion blender to blend the soup until smooth. Alternatively, transfer the soup to a blender and blend in batches until smooth.
5. Return the soup to the pot over low heat. Stir in shredded cheddar cheese until melted and smooth.
6. Pour in heavy cream and stir until well combined. Let the soup simmer for another 5 minutes.
7. Ladle the rich and velvety broccoli cheese soup into serving bowls. Garnish with crispy bacon bits if desired.
8. Serve hot and enjoy this indulgent and comforting broccoli cheese soup!

Nutritional Info (per serving): Calories: 320 | Fat: 25g | Carbs: 8g | Protein: 15g

Atkins Diet Feature: This broccoli cheese soup is low in carbs and packed with protein and healthy fats, making it a perfect choice for the Atkins Diet. The creamy texture and cheesy flavor make it a satisfying meal option!

Creamy Cauliflower Soup with Crispy Bacon

Prep: 15 mins | Cook: 25 mins | Serves: 4

Ingredients:
- 1 head cauliflower, chopped into florets (about 600g)
- 2 tablespoons olive oil (30ml)
- 1 onion, chopped (1 onion)
- 2 cloves garlic, minced (2 cloves)
- 4 cups chicken or vegetable broth (960ml)
- Salt and pepper to taste
- 1/2 cup heavy cream (120ml)
- Crispy bacon bits for garnish (optional)
- Chopped chives for garnish (optional)

Instructions:
1. Preheat your oven to 400°F (200°C). Place cauliflower florets on a baking sheet, drizzle with olive oil, and season with salt and pepper. Roast in the preheated oven for 2025 minutes until golden and tender.
2. In a large pot, heat olive oil over medium heat. Add chopped onion and minced garlic. Sauté until softened and fragrant, about 5 minutes.
3. Add roasted cauliflower to the pot and pour in chicken or vegetable broth. Bring to a boil, then reduce the heat and let it simmer for 10 minutes.
4. Use an immersion blender to blend the soup until smooth. Alternatively, transfer the soup to a blender and blend in batches until smooth.
5. Return the soup to the pot over low heat. Stir in heavy cream until well combined. Let the soup simmer for another 5 minutes.
6. Ladle the creamy cauliflower soup into serving bowls. Garnish with crispy bacon bits and chopped chives if desired.
7. Serve hot and enjoy this creamy and nutritious cauliflower soup!

Nutritional Info (per serving): Calories: 280 | Fat: 20g | Carbs: 10g | Protein: 10g

Atkins Diet Feature: This creamy cauliflower soup is low in carbs and high in fiber, making it suitable for the Atkins Diet. The addition of heavy cream provides richness, while crispy bacon adds a delightful crunch!

Hearty Taco Soup with Ground Beef

Prep: 15 mins | Cook: 25 mins | Serves: 4

Ingredients:
- 1 lb ground beef (450g)
- 1 onion, chopped (1 onion)
- 2 cloves garlic, minced (2 cloves)
- 1 bell pepper, diced (1 pepper)
- 1 can (14 oz) diced tomatoes (400g)
- 1 can (4 oz) diced green chilies (120g)
- 2 cups beef broth (480ml)
- 1 tablespoon chili powder (15g)
- 1 teaspoon ground cumin (5g)
- Salt and pepper to taste
- Avocado slices for garnish (optional)
- Shredded cheese for garnish (optional)
- Chopped fresh cilantro for garnish (optional)

Instructions:
1. In a large pot, brown the ground beef over medium heat until fully cooked. Drain any excess fat.
2. Add chopped onion, minced garlic, and diced bell pepper to the pot. Sauté until softened, about 5 minutes.
3. Stir in diced tomatoes, diced green chilies, beef broth, chili powder, and ground cumin. Season with salt and pepper to taste.
4. Bring the mixture to a simmer and let it cook for 15 minutes, allowing the flavors to meld together.
5. Taste and adjust seasoning if needed.
6. Ladle the hearty taco soup into serving bowls.
7. Garnish with avocado slices, shredded cheese, and chopped fresh cilantro if desired.
8. Serve hot and enjoy this flavorful and satisfying taco soup!

Nutritional Info (per serving): Calories: 320 | Fat: 20g | Carbs: 10g | Protein: 25g

Atkins Diet Feature: This hearty taco soup is low in carbs and high in protein, making it a perfect choice for the Atkins Diet. It's packed with flavor and can be customized with your favorite toppings!

Classic Italian Wedding Soup

Prep: 20 mins | Cook: 30 mins | Serves: 4

Ingredients:
- 1 tablespoon olive oil (15ml)
- 1 onion, chopped (1 onion)
- 2 carrots, diced (2 carrots)
- 2 stalks celery, diced (2 stalks)
- 2 cloves garlic, minced (2 cloves)
- 6 cups chicken broth (1440ml)
- 8 oz lean ground beef or turkey (225g)
- 1/4 cup grated Parmesan cheese (25g)
- 1/4 cup chopped fresh parsley (15g)
- 1 egg, beaten
- Salt and pepper to taste
- Baby spinach leaves for serving

Instructions:
1. In a large pot, heat olive oil over medium heat. Add chopped onion, diced carrots, diced celery, and minced garlic. Sauté until softened, about 5 minutes.
2. Pour in chicken broth and bring to a simmer.
3. Meanwhile, in a bowl, mix together ground beef or turkey, grated Parmesan cheese, chopped fresh parsley, beaten egg, salt, and pepper until well combined.
4. Form the mixture into small meatballs, about 1 inch in diameter.
5. Gently drop the meatballs into the simmering broth and let them cook for 10 minutes until cooked through.
6. Taste and adjust seasoning if needed.
7. Add baby spinach leaves to the pot and let them wilt for 12 minutes.

8. Ladle the classic Italian wedding soup into serving bowls.
9. Serve hot and enjoy this comforting and nutritious soup!

Nutritional Info (per serving): Calories: 250 | Fat: 10g | Carbs: 10g | Protein: 20g

Atkins Diet Feature: This classic Italian wedding soup is low in carbs and packed with protein, making it a perfect choice for the Atkins Diet. The combination of savory meatballs, flavorful broth, and nutritious vegetables is simply delightful!

Classic Chili with Beef and Beans

Prep: 20 mins | Cook: 1 hour 30 mins | Serves: 6

Ingredients:
- 1 tablespoon olive oil (15ml)
- 1 onion, chopped (1 onion)
- 2 cloves garlic, minced (2 cloves)
- 1 lb ground beef (450g)
- 1 can (14 oz) diced tomatoes (400g)
- 1 can (14 oz) tomato sauce (400g)
- 1 can (14 oz) kidney beans, drained and rinsed (400g)
- 1 can (14 oz) black beans, drained and rinsed (400g)
- 1 tablespoon chili powder (15g)
- 1 teaspoon ground cumin (5g)
- Salt and pepper to taste
- Shredded cheddar cheese for garnish (optional)
- Chopped fresh cilantro for garnish (optional)
- Sour cream for serving (optional)

Instructions:
1. In a large pot, heat olive oil over medium heat. Add chopped onion and minced garlic. Sauté until softened, about 5 minutes.
2. Add ground beef to the pot. Cook until browned and cooked through, breaking it into small pieces with a spoon, about 710 minutes.

3. Stir in diced tomatoes, tomato sauce, kidney beans, black beans, chili powder, and ground cumin. Season with salt and pepper to taste.
4. Bring the chili to a simmer. Reduce the heat to low, cover, and let it simmer for 1 hour, stirring occasionally.
5. Taste and adjust seasoning if needed.
6. Ladle the classic chili into serving bowls.
7. Garnish with shredded cheddar cheese, chopped fresh cilantro, and a dollop of sour cream if desired.
8. Serve hot and enjoy this comforting and flavorful chili!

Nutritional Info (per serving): Calories: 350 | Fat: 15g | Carbs: 25g | Protein: 20g

Atkins Diet Feature: This classic chili is moderate in carbs and high in protein, making it a suitable option for the Atkins Diet. It's a hearty and satisfying dish that's perfect for chilly nights!

Creamy Clam Chowder

Prep: 20 mins | Cook: 30 mins | Serves: 4

Ingredients:
- 4 slices bacon, chopped (4 slices)
- 1 onion, chopped (1 onion)
- 2 stalks celery, diced (2 stalks)
- 2 cloves garlic, minced (2 cloves)
- 2 tablespoons butter (30g)
- 2 tablespoons allpurpose flour (30g)
- 2 cups chicken broth (480ml)
- 2 cups halfandhalf (480ml)
- 2 cans (6.5 oz each) chopped clams, drained, juices reserved (2 cans, 185g each)
- 2 large potatoes, peeled and diced (2 potatoes)
- 1 bay leaf
- Salt and pepper to taste
- Chopped fresh parsley for garnish (optional)
- Oyster crackers for serving (optional)

1. In a large pot, cook chopped bacon over medium heat until crispy. Remove bacon from the pot and set aside, leaving the drippings in the pot.
2. Add chopped onion, diced celery, and minced garlic to the pot with the bacon drippings. Sauté until softened, about 5 minutes.
3. Add butter to the pot and let it melt. Stir in allpurpose flour to form a roux. Cook for 23 minutes until golden.
4. Gradually pour in chicken broth and halfandhalf, stirring constantly to prevent lumps from forming.
5. Add chopped clams (reserving the juices), diced potatoes, bay leaf, and reserved clam juices to the pot. Season with salt and pepper to taste.
6. Bring the chowder to a simmer. Cover and let it cook for 1520 minutes, or until the potatoes are tender, stirring occasionally.
7. Taste and adjust seasoning if needed.
8. Ladle the creamy clam chowder into serving bowls.
9. Garnish with crispy bacon pieces and chopped fresh parsley if desired.
10. Serve hot with oyster crackers on the side if desired.
11. Enjoy this creamy and comforting clam chowder!

Nutritional Info (per serving): Calories: 400 | Fat: 20g | Carbs: 30g | Protein: 15g

Atkins Diet Feature: This creamy clam chowder is moderate in carbs and can fit into the Atkins Diet, especially if enjoyed in moderation. It's a rich and satisfying soup that's perfect for a cozy meal!

Homemade Chicken Noodle Soup

Prep: 15 mins | Cook: 30 mins | Serves: 4

Ingredients:
- 1 tablespoon olive oil (15ml)
- 1 onion, chopped (1 onion)
- 2 carrots, diced (2 carrots)
- 2 stalks celery, diced (2 stalks)
- 2 cloves garlic, minced (2 cloves)
- 4 cups chicken broth (960ml)

- 2 cups cooked chicken, shredded (300g)
- 1 cup uncooked lowcarb noodles (such as shirataki noodles or zucchini noodles) (about 100g)
- 1 teaspoon dried thyme (5g)
- Salt and pepper to taste
- Chopped fresh parsley for garnish (optional)
- Lemon wedges for serving (optional)

Instructions:

1. In a large pot, heat olive oil over medium heat. Add chopped onion, diced carrots, diced celery, and minced garlic. Sauté until softened, about 5 minutes.

2. Pour in chicken broth and bring to a simmer.

3. Add shredded cooked chicken, uncooked lowcarb noodles, and dried thyme to the pot. Season with salt and pepper to taste.

4. Let the soup simmer for 1520 minutes, or until the noodles are tender and cooked through.

5. Taste and adjust seasoning if needed.

6. Ladle the homemade chicken noodle soup into serving bowls.

7. Garnish with chopped fresh parsley and serve with lemon wedges on the side if desired.

8. Serve hot and enjoy this comforting and nourishing soup!

Nutritional Info (per serving): Calories: 250 | Fat: 10g | Carbs: 15g | Protein: 20g

Atkins Diet Feature: This homemade chicken noodle soup is moderate in carbs and high in protein, making it a suitable option for the Atkins Diet. It's a classic and comforting soup that's perfect for any time of the year!

Hearty Beef and Veggie Stew

Prep: 20 mins | Cook: 1 hour 30 mins | Serves: 4

Ingredients:
- 1 lb stewing beef, cut into cubes (450g)
- 2 tablespoons olive oil (30ml)
- 1 onion, chopped (1 onion)
- 2 cloves garlic, minced (2 cloves)
- 2 carrots, diced (2 carrots)
- 2 stalks celery, diced (2 stalks)
- 2 cups beef broth (480ml)
- 1 can (14 oz) diced tomatoes (400g)
- 1 tablespoon tomato paste (15g)
- 1 teaspoon dried thyme (5g)
- 1 teaspoon dried rosemary (5g)
- Salt and pepper to taste
- Chopped fresh parsley for garnish (optional)

Instructions:
1. In a large pot, heat olive oil over medium heat. Add cubed stewing beef and brown on all sides, about 5 minutes.
2. Add chopped onion, minced garlic, diced carrots, and diced celery to the pot. Sauté until softened, about 5 minutes.
3. Pour in beef broth, diced tomatoes, tomato paste, dried thyme, and dried rosemary. Season with salt and pepper to taste.
4. Bring the mixture to a simmer, then reduce the heat to low. Cover and let it cook for 1 hour, stirring occasionally.
5. Taste and adjust seasoning if needed.
6. Serve hot, garnished with chopped fresh parsley if desired.
7. Enjoy this hearty beef and veggie stew as a comforting and nutritious meal!

Nutritional Info (per serving): Calories: 350 | Fat: 15g | Carbs: 10g | Protein: 30g

Atkins Diet Feature: This hearty beef and veggie stew is low in carbs and high in protein, making it a satisfying meal option for the Atkins Diet. It's packed with tender beef, flavorful vegetables, and aromatic herbs!

Prep: 15 mins | Cook: 1 hour | Serves: 4

Ingredients:
- 2 lbs fresh tomatoes, halved (about 900g)
- 4 cloves garlic, peeled (4 cloves)
- 2 tablespoons olive oil (30ml)
- Salt and pepper to taste
- 1 onion, chopped (1 onion)
- 2 cups vegetable broth (480ml)
- 1/4 cup chopped fresh basil leaves (15g)
- 1/4 cup heavy cream (60ml)
- Grated Parmesan cheese for garnish (optional)
- Croutons for garnish (optional)

Instructions:
1. Preheat your oven to 400°F (200°C). Place halved tomatoes and peeled garlic cloves on a baking sheet. Drizzle with olive oil and season with salt and pepper. Roast in the preheated oven for 3040 minutes until caramelized.
2. In a large pot, heat olive oil over medium heat. Add chopped onion and sauté until softened, about 5 minutes.
3. Add roasted tomatoes and garlic to the pot, along with any juices from the baking sheet. Pour in vegetable broth and bring to a simmer.
4. Let the mixture cook for 2030 minutes, allowing the flavors to meld together.
5. Use an immersion blender to blend the soup until smooth. Alternatively, transfer the soup to a blender and blend in batches until smooth.
6. Stir in chopped fresh basil leaves and heavy cream. Let the soup simmer for another 5 minutes.
7. Taste and adjust seasoning if needed.
8. Ladle the roasted tomato basil soup into serving bowls.
9. Garnish with grated Parmesan cheese and croutons if desired.
10.   Serve hot and enjoy this comforting and flavorful soup!

Nutritional Info (per serving): Calories: 200 | Fat: 15g | Carbs: 15g | Protein: 5g

Atkins Diet Feature: This roasted tomato basil soup is low in carbs and packed with flavor, making it a perfect choice for the Atkins Diet. The combination of roasted tomatoes, garlic, and fresh basil creates a deliciously aromatic soup that's both comforting and nutritious!

Spicy Buffalo Chicken Soup

Prep: 15 mins | Cook: 30 mins | Serves: 4

Ingredients:
- 2 tablespoons butter (30g)
- 1 onion, chopped (1 onion)
- 2 cloves garlic, minced (2 cloves)
- 2 cups cooked chicken, shredded (300g)
- 4 cups chicken broth (960ml)
- 1/2 cup hot sauce (120ml)
- 1/4 cup heavy cream (60ml)
- Salt and pepper to taste
- Blue cheese crumbles for garnish (optional)
- Chopped green onions for garnish (optional)
- Celery sticks for serving (optional)

Instructions:
1. In a large pot, melt butter over medium heat. Add chopped onion and minced garlic. Sauté until softened, about 5 minutes.
2. Add shredded cooked chicken to the pot and stir to combine.
3. Pour in chicken broth and bring to a simmer.
4. Stir in hot sauce and heavy cream. Season with salt and pepper to taste.
5. Let the soup simmer for 2025 minutes, allowing the flavors to meld together.
6. Taste and adjust seasoning if needed.
7. Ladle the spicy buffalo chicken soup into serving bowls.
8. Garnish with blue cheese crumbles and chopped green onions if desired.
9. Serve hot with celery sticks on the side for dipping, if desired.
10.   Enjoy this spicy and satisfying buffalo chicken soup!

Nutritional Info (per serving): Calories: 250 | Fat: 15g | Carbs: 5g | Protein: 20g

Atkins Diet Feature: This spicy buffalo chicken soup is low in carbs and high in protein, making it a perfect choice for the Atkins Diet. The combination of tender chicken, spicy hot sauce, and creamy broth creates a flavor explosion that's sure to please your taste buds!

Creamy Tuna Noodle Casserole Soup

Prep: 15 mins | Cook: 30 mins | Serves: 4

Ingredients:
- 2 tablespoons butter (30g)
- 1 onion, chopped (1 onion)
- 2 cloves garlic, minced (2 cloves)
- 2 cups sliced mushrooms (about 200g)
- 1/4 cup allpurpose flour (30g)
- 4 cups chicken broth (960ml)
- 1 cup heavy cream (240ml)
- 2 cans (5 oz each) tuna, drained (2 cans, 140g each)
- 2 cups cooked lowcarb pasta (such as shirataki noodles or zucchini noodles) (about 200g)
- Salt and pepper to taste
- Chopped fresh parsley for garnish (optional)
- Grated Parmesan cheese for garnish (optional)

Instructions:
1. In a large pot, melt butter over medium heat. Add chopped onion and minced garlic. Sauté until softened, about 5 minutes.
2. Add sliced mushrooms to the pot and cook until they release their juices, about 5 minutes.
3. Sprinkle allpurpose flour over the mushroom mixture and stir to combine. Cook for 23 minutes until the flour is golden.
4. Pour in chicken broth and heavy cream. Bring to a simmer.
5. Stir in drained tuna and cooked lowcarb pasta. Season with salt and pepper to taste.
6. Let the soup simmer for 1520 minutes, allowing the flavors to meld together.
7. Taste and adjust seasoning if needed.
8. Ladle the creamy tuna noodle casserole soup into serving bowls.

9. Garnish with chopped fresh parsley and grated Parmesan cheese if desired.
10. Serve hot and enjoy this comforting and creamy soup!

Nutritional Info (per serving): Calories: 350 | Fat: 25g | Carbs: 10g | Protein: 20g

Atkins Diet Feature: This creamy tuna noodle casserole soup is low in carbs and high in protein, making it a suitable option for the Atkins Diet. It's a comforting and satisfying meal that's reminiscent of the classic casserole dish but in a soup form!

Flavorful Cabbage Roll Soup

Prep: 20 mins | Cook: 45 mins | Serves: 4

Ingredients:
- 1 lb ground beef (450g)
- 1 onion, chopped (1 onion)
- 2 cloves garlic, minced (2 cloves)
- 4 cups beef broth (960ml)
- 1 can (14 oz) diced tomatoes (400g)
- 2 cups shredded cabbage (about 200g)
- 1 cup cauliflower rice (about 100g)
- 1 teaspoon paprika (5g)
- 1 teaspoon dried thyme (5g)
- Salt and pepper to taste
- Chopped fresh parsley for garnish (optional)
- Sour cream for serving (optional)

Instructions:
1. In a large pot, brown the ground beef over medium heat until fully cooked. Drain any excess fat.
2. Add chopped onion and minced garlic to the pot. Sauté until softened, about 5 minutes.
3. Pour in beef broth and diced tomatoes with their juices. Stir to combine.

4. Add shredded cabbage and cauliflower rice to the pot. Season with paprika, dried thyme, salt, and pepper.
5. Bring the soup to a simmer and let it cook for 3040 minutes, allowing the flavors to meld together and the cabbage to soften.
6. Taste and adjust seasoning if needed.
7. Ladle the flavorful cabbage roll soup into serving bowls.
8. Garnish with chopped fresh parsley and a dollop of sour cream if desired.
9. Serve hot and enjoy this delicious and nutritious soup!

Nutritional Info (per serving): Calories: 300 | Fat: 20g | Carbs: 10g | Protein: 20g

Atkins Diet Feature: This flavorful cabbage roll soup is low in carbs and high in protein, making it a great option for the Atkins Diet. It's a hearty and satisfying soup that's packed with cabbage, ground beef, and aromatic spices!

Hearty Ham and Bean Soup

Prep: 15 mins | Cook: 1 hour 30 mins | Serves: 4

Ingredients:
- 1 tablespoon olive oil (15ml)
- 1 onion, chopped (1 onion)
- 2 carrots, diced (2 carrots)
- 2 stalks celery, diced (2 stalks)
- 2 cloves garlic, minced (2 cloves)
- 1 ham hock or 1 cup diced ham (about 225g)
- 4 cups chicken or vegetable broth (960ml)
- 2 cans (15 oz each) cannellini beans, drained and rinsed (2 cans, 420g each)
- 1 bay leaf
- Salt and pepper to taste
- Chopped fresh parsley for garnish (optional)

Instructions:

1. In a large pot, heat olive oil over medium heat. Add chopped onion, diced carrots, diced celery, and minced garlic. Sauté until softened, about 5 minutes.
2. Add the ham hock or diced ham to the pot. Pour in chicken or vegetable broth.
3. Add drained and rinsed cannellini beans and bay leaf to the pot. Season with salt and pepper to taste.
4. Bring the soup to a simmer, then reduce the heat to low. Cover and let it cook for 1 hour, stirring occasionally.
5. After 1 hour, remove the ham hock from the soup and shred the meat. Discard the bone and any excess fat.
6. Return the shredded ham to the pot and let the soup simmer for another 30 minutes, allowing the flavors to meld together.
7. Taste and adjust seasoning if needed.
8. Ladle the hearty ham and bean soup into serving bowls.
9. Garnish with chopped fresh parsley if desired.
10.   Serve hot and enjoy this comforting and nutritious soup!

Nutritional Info (per serving): Calories: 280 | Fat: 10g | Carbs: 25g | Protein: 20g

Atkins Diet Feature: This hearty ham and bean soup is moderate in carbs and high in protein, making it suitable for the Atkins Diet. It's a satisfying and flavorful soup that's perfect for cold days!

Satisfying Sausage and Kale Soup

Prep: 15 mins | Cook: 30 mins | Serves: 4

Ingredients:
- 1 tablespoon olive oil (15ml)
- 1 lb Italian sausage, casings removed (about 450g)
- 1 onion, chopped (1 onion)
- 2 cloves garlic, minced (2 cloves)
- 4 cups chicken broth (960ml)
- 1 can (14 oz) diced tomatoes (400g)
- 4 cups chopped kale leaves (about 200g)

- 1 teaspoon dried oregano (5g)
- Salt and pepper to taste
- Grated Parmesan cheese for garnish (optional)
- Crushed red pepper flakes for garnish (optional)

Instructions:

1. In a large pot, heat olive oil over medium heat. Add Italian sausage, breaking it into small pieces with a spoon. Cook until browned and cooked through, about 57 minutes.
2. Add chopped onion and minced garlic to the pot. Sauté until softened, about 5 minutes.
3. Pour in chicken broth and diced tomatoes with their juices. Stir to combine.
4. Add chopped kale leaves and dried oregano to the pot. Season with salt and pepper to taste.
5. Bring the soup to a simmer and let it cook for 1520 minutes, allowing the flavors to meld together and the kale to wilt.
6. Taste and adjust seasoning if needed.
7. Ladle the satisfying sausage and kale soup into serving bowls.
8. Garnish with grated Parmesan cheese and crushed red pepper flakes if desired.
9. Serve hot and enjoy this hearty and nutritious soup!

Nutritional Info (per serving): Calories: 350 | Fat: 25g | Carbs: 10g | Protein: 20g

Atkins Diet Feature: This satisfying sausage and kale soup is low in carbs and high in protein, making it a great option for the Atkins Diet. It's packed with flavorful Italian sausage, nutritious kale, and aromatic spices!

CHAPTER FIVE: POULTRY MAIN DISHES

Bacon Wrapped Chicken Breast

Prep: 10 mins | Cook: 25 mins | Serves: 4

Ingredients:
- 4 boneless, skinless chicken breasts (about 600g)
- 8 slices bacon (8 slices)
- Salt and pepper to taste
- 1 teaspoon garlic powder (5g)
- 1 teaspoon paprika (5g)
- 1 tablespoon olive oil (15ml)

Instructions:
1. Preheat your oven to 400°F (200°C).
2. Season chicken breasts with salt, pepper, garlic powder, and paprika.
3. Wrap each chicken breast with 2 slices of bacon, securing with toothpicks if necessary.
4. Heat olive oil in an ovensafe skillet over mediumhigh heat.
5. Sear the baconwrapped chicken breasts in the skillet until the bacon is crispy, about 34 minutes per side.
6. Transfer the skillet to the preheated oven and bake for 1520 minutes, or until the chicken is cooked through and reaches an internal temperature of 165°F (75°C).
7. Remove from the oven and let it rest for a few minutes before serving.
8. Serve hot and enjoy this savory baconwrapped chicken!

Nutritional Info (per serving): Calories: 350 | Fat: 20g | Carbs: 0g | Protein: 40g

Atkins Diet Feature: This baconwrapped chicken breast is a proteinrich dish suitable for the Atkins Diet. It's flavorful, easy to make, and perfect for a satisfying meal!

Chicken Parmesan

Prep: 15 mins | Cook: 25 mins | Serves: 4

Ingredients:
- 4 boneless, skinless chicken breasts (about 600g)
- 1 cup almond flour (100g)
- 1/2 cup grated Parmesan cheese (50g)
- 1 teaspoon Italian seasoning (5g)
- Salt and pepper to taste
- 2 eggs, beaten
- 1 cup sugarfree marinara sauce (240ml)
- 1 cup shredded mozzarella cheese (100g)
- Fresh basil leaves for garnish (optional)

Instructions:
1. Preheat your oven to 400°F (200°C).
2. In a shallow dish, combine almond flour, grated Parmesan cheese, Italian seasoning, salt, and pepper.
3. Dip each chicken breast in beaten eggs, then dredge in the almond flour mixture, pressing to coat evenly.
4. Heat olive oil in a large skillet over mediumhigh heat.
5. Add chicken breasts to the skillet and cook until golden brown on both sides, about 34 minutes per side.
6. Transfer the browned chicken breasts to a baking dish.
7. Spoon marinara sauce over each chicken breast, then sprinkle with shredded mozzarella cheese.
8. Bake in the preheated oven for 1520 minutes, or until the chicken is cooked through and the cheese is melted and bubbly.
9. Remove from the oven and let it rest for a few minutes before serving.
10. Garnish with fresh basil leaves if desired.
11. Serve hot and enjoy this delicious chicken Parmesan!

Nutritional Info (per serving): Calories: 380 | Fat: 20g | Carbs: 10g | Protein: 40g

Atkins Diet Feature: This chicken Parmesan recipe uses almond flour instead of breadcrumbs, making it low in carbs and suitable for the Atkins Diet. It's a flavorful and satisfying dish that's sure to please everyone at the table!

Prep: 15 mins | Cook: 20 mins | Serves: 4

Ingredients:
- 1 lb ground chicken (about 450g)
- 1/4 cup almond flour (30g)
- 1/4 cup grated Parmesan cheese (25g)
- 1 large egg
- 1/4 cup hot sauce (60ml)
- 2 tablespoons unsalted butter, melted (30g)
- 1 teaspoon garlic powder (5g)
- Salt and pepper to taste
- Ranch dressing for serving (optional)
- Celery sticks for serving (optional)

Instructions:
1. Preheat your oven to 400°F (200°C). Line a baking sheet with parchment paper.
2. In a large bowl, combine ground chicken, almond flour, grated Parmesan cheese, egg, hot sauce, melted butter, garlic powder, salt, and pepper. Mix until well combined.
3. Using your hands, shape the mixture into golf ballsized meatballs and place them on the prepared baking sheet.
4. Bake in the preheated oven for 1520 minutes, or until the meatballs are cooked through and golden brown.
5. Remove from the oven and let them cool slightly before serving.
6. Serve hot buffalo chicken meatballs with ranch dressing and celery sticks on the side, if desired.
7. Enjoy these flavorful and spicy meatballs as a tasty appetizer or main dish!

Nutritional Info (per serving): Calories: 320 | Fat: 20g | Carbs: 5g | Protein: 30g

Atkins Diet Feature: These buffalo chicken meatballs are low in carbs and high in protein, making them a perfect choice for the Atkins Diet. They're packed with flavor and are sure to be a hit at any gathering!

Chicken Fajitas

Prep: 15 mins | Cook: 15 mins | Serves: 4

Ingredients:
- 1 lb boneless, skinless chicken breasts (about 450g), thinly sliced
- 2 bell peppers, thinly sliced (2 peppers)
- 1 onion, thinly sliced (1 onion)
- 2 tablespoons olive oil (30ml)
- 2 tablespoons fajita seasoning (30g)
- Salt and pepper to taste
- 8 lowcarb tortillas, warmed (or lettuce leaves for a lowcarb option)
- Optional toppings: shredded cheese, sour cream, salsa, guacamole

Instructions:
1. In a large bowl, toss the sliced chicken breasts, bell peppers, and onion with olive oil and fajita seasoning until evenly coated.
2. Heat a large skillet over mediumhigh heat. Add the seasoned chicken, bell peppers, and onion to the skillet.
3. Cook, stirring occasionally, until the chicken is cooked through and the vegetables are tender, about 810 minutes.
4. Season with salt and pepper to taste.
5. Remove from heat and serve the chicken fajitas on warmed tortillas or lettuce leaves.
6. Serve hot with your choice of toppings such as shredded cheese, sour cream, salsa, or guacamole.
7. Enjoy these delicious and flavorful chicken fajitas!

Nutritional Info (per serving, excluding toppings): Calories: 300 | Fat: 12g | Carbs: 15g | Protein: 30g

Atkins Diet Feature: These chicken fajitas are low in carbs and high in protein, making them suitable for the Atkins Diet. They're a quick and easy meal option that's packed with TexMex flavors!

Chicken Cordon Bleu

Prep: 20 mins | Cook: 25 mins | Serves: 4

Ingredients:
- 4 boneless, skinless chicken breasts (about 600g)
- Salt and pepper to taste
- 4 slices deli ham (4 slices)
- 4 slices Swiss cheese (4 slices)
- 1/2 cup almond flour (50g)
- 1/4 cup grated Parmesan cheese (25g)
- 1 teaspoon garlic powder (5g)
- 2 large eggs, beaten
- 2 tablespoons olive oil (30ml)

Instructions:
1. Preheat your oven to 375°F (190°C). Grease a baking dish with olive oil or nonstick cooking spray.
2. Place each chicken breast between two sheets of plastic wrap. Use a meat mallet or rolling pin to pound the chicken to an even thickness, about 1/4 inch.
3. Season each chicken breast with salt and pepper to taste.
4. Place a slice of ham and a slice of Swiss cheese on top of each chicken breast.
5. Starting with the short end, roll up each chicken breast tightly and secure with toothpicks.
6. In a shallow dish, combine almond flour, grated Parmesan cheese, and garlic powder.
7. Dip each chicken rollup in beaten eggs, then dredge in the almond flour mixture, pressing to coat evenly.
8. Heat olive oil in a large skillet over mediumhigh heat.
9. Sear the chicken rollups in the skillet until golden brown on all sides, about 23 minutes per side.
10.   Transfer the seared chicken rollups to the prepared baking dish.
11.   Bake in the preheated oven for 2025 minutes, or until the chicken is cooked through and the cheese is melted and bubbly.
12.   Remove from the oven and let them cool slightly before serving.
13.   Serve hot and enjoy this classic chicken cordon bleu!

Nutritional Info (per serving): Calories: 400 | Fat: 25g | Carbs: 5g | Protein: 40g

Atkins Diet Feature: This chicken cordon bleu recipe uses almond flour instead of breadcrumbs, making it low in carbs and suitable for the Atkins Diet. It's a delicious and elegant dish that's perfect for a special occasion or a family dinner!

Lemon Garlic Roasted Chicken

Prep: 10 mins | Cook: 45 mins | Serves: 4

Ingredients:
- 4 bonein, skinon chicken thighs (about 600g)
- 2 tablespoons olive oil (30ml)
- 2 cloves garlic, minced (2 cloves)
- Zest and juice of 1 lemon
- 1 teaspoon dried thyme (5g)
- Salt and pepper to taste
- Fresh parsley for garnish (optional)

Instructions:
1. Preheat your oven to 400°F (200°C). Line a baking sheet with parchment paper.
2. In a small bowl, whisk together olive oil, minced garlic, lemon zest, lemon juice, dried thyme, salt, and pepper.
3. Place the chicken thighs on the prepared baking sheet.
4. Brush the lemon garlic mixture over the chicken thighs, coating them evenly.
5. Roast in the preheated oven for 4045 minutes, or until the chicken is golden brown and cooked through, with an internal temperature of 165°F (75°C).
6. Remove from the oven and let the chicken rest for a few minutes before serving.
7. Garnish with fresh parsley if desired.
8. Serve hot and enjoy this flavorful lemon garlic roasted chicken!

Nutritional Info (per serving): Calories: 350 | Fat: 25g | Carbs: 1g | Protein: 30g

Atkins Diet Feature: This lemon garlic roasted chicken is low in carbs and high in protein, making it a perfect option for the Atkins Diet. It's a simple and delicious dish that's bursting with citrusy and aromatic flavors!

BBQ Chicken Drumsticks

Prep: 10 mins | Cook: 35 mins | Serves: 4

Ingredients:
- 8 chicken drumsticks (about 800g)
- 1 cup sugarfree barbecue sauce (240ml)
- 2 tablespoons olive oil (30ml)
- 1 teaspoon smoked paprika (5g)
- 1 teaspoon garlic powder (5g)
- Salt and pepper to taste
- Chopped fresh parsley for garnish (optional)

Instructions:
1. Preheat your oven to 400°F (200°C). Line a baking sheet with parchment paper.
2. In a bowl, mix together barbecue sauce, olive oil, smoked paprika, garlic powder, salt, and pepper.
3. Place the chicken drumsticks in a large resealable plastic bag or a bowl.
4. Pour the barbecue sauce mixture over the chicken drumsticks, making sure they are evenly coated. Marinate for at least 30 minutes, or overnight in the refrigerator for more flavor.
5. Arrange the chicken drumsticks on the prepared baking sheet, leaving space between each piece.
6. Bake in the preheated oven for 3035 minutes, or until the chicken is cooked through and the skin is crispy, brushing with additional barbecue sauce halfway through cooking.
7. Remove from the oven and let them rest for a few minutes before serving.
8. Garnish with chopped fresh parsley if desired.
9. Serve hot and enjoy these fingerlicking BBQ chicken drumsticks!

Nutritional Info (per serving): Calories: 320 | Fat: 15g | Carbs: 5g | Protein: 30g

Atkins Diet Feature: These BBQ chicken drumsticks are low in carbs and high in protein, making them a great option for the Atkins Diet. They're tender, juicy, and packed with smoky barbecue flavor!

Chicken Enchiladas

Prep: 20 mins | Cook: 25 mins | Serves: 4

Ingredients:
- 1 lb cooked chicken, shredded (about 450g)
- 8 lowcarb tortillas (or lettuce leaves for a lowcarb option)
- 1 cup sugarfree enchilada sauce (240ml)
- 1 cup shredded cheddar cheese (100g)
- 1/2 cup diced onion (1/2 onion)
- 1/2 cup diced bell pepper (1/2 pepper)
- 2 cloves garlic, minced (2 cloves)
- 1 teaspoon chili powder (5g)
- 1 teaspoon ground cumin (5g)
- Salt and pepper to taste
- Chopped fresh cilantro for garnish (optional)
- Sour cream for serving (optional)
- Sliced jalapenos for serving (optional)

Instructions:
1. Preheat your oven to 375°F (190°C). Grease a baking dish with olive oil or nonstick cooking spray.
2. In a skillet, heat olive oil over medium heat. Add diced onion, diced bell pepper, and minced garlic. Sauté until softened, about 5 minutes.
3. Add shredded chicken, chili powder, ground cumin, salt, and pepper to the skillet. Cook for an additional 23 minutes to heat through and combine flavors.
4. Warm the lowcarb tortillas according to package instructions.
5. Spread a spoonful of enchilada sauce onto each tortilla.
6. Spoon the chicken mixture onto each tortilla, then sprinkle with shredded cheddar cheese.

7. Roll up the tortillas and place them seamside down in the prepared baking dish.
8. Pour the remaining enchilada sauce over the rolled tortillas.
9. Sprinkle additional shredded cheddar cheese on top.
10. Bake in the preheated oven for 2025 minutes, or until the cheese is melted and bubbly.
11. Remove from the oven and let them cool slightly before serving.
12. Garnish with chopped fresh cilantro if desired.
13. Serve hot with sour cream and sliced jalapenos on the side if desired.
14. Enjoy these delicious and satisfying chicken enchiladas!

Nutritional Info (per serving): Calories: 350 | Fat: 20g | Carbs: 15g | Protein: 30g

Atkins Diet Feature: These chicken enchiladas use lowcarb tortillas and sugarfree enchilada sauce, making them suitable for the Atkins Diet. They're packed with TexMex flavors and are sure to be a family favorite!

Pesto Chicken Casserole

Prep: 15 mins | Cook: 35 mins | Serves: 4

Ingredients:
- 4 boneless, skinless chicken breasts (about 600g)
- Salt and pepper to taste
- 1/2 cup sugarfree basil pesto (120ml)
- 1 cup shredded mozzarella cheese (100g)
- 1/4 cup grated Parmesan cheese (25g)
- 1/4 cup almond flour (30g)
- 2 tablespoons olive oil (30ml)
- Fresh basil leaves for garnish (optional)

Instructions:
1. Preheat your oven to 375°F (190°C). Grease a baking dish with olive oil or nonstick cooking spray.
2. Season the chicken breasts with salt and pepper to taste.

3. In a bowl, mix together sugarfree basil pesto, shredded mozzarella cheese, grated Parmesan cheese, almond flour, and olive oil until well combined.
4. Place the seasoned chicken breasts in the prepared baking dish.
5. Spread the pesto mixture evenly over the chicken breasts.
6. Bake in the preheated oven for 3035 minutes, or until the chicken is cooked through and the cheese is melted and bubbly.
7. Remove from the oven and let them cool slightly before serving.
8. Garnish with fresh basil leaves if desired.
9. Serve hot and enjoy this flavorful and creamy pesto chicken casserole!

Nutritional Info (per serving): Calories: 400 | Fat: 25g | Carbs: 2g | Protein: 40g

Atkins Diet Feature: This pesto chicken casserole is low in carbs and high in protein, making it suitable for the Atkins Diet. It's a delicious and comforting dish that's easy to make and perfect for a weeknight dinner!

Chicken Piccata

Prep: 15 mins | Cook: 20 mins | Serves: 4

Ingredients:
- 4 boneless, skinless chicken breasts (about 600g)
- Salt and pepper to taste
- 1/2 cup almond flour (50g)
- 1/4 cup grated Parmesan cheese (25g)
- 2 tablespoons unsalted butter (30g)
- 2 tablespoons olive oil (30ml)
- 2 cloves garlic, minced (2 cloves)
- 1/2 cup chicken broth (120ml)
- 1/4 cup fresh lemon juice (60ml)
- 1/4 cup capers, drained (30g)
- 2 tablespoons chopped fresh parsley for garnish (optional)
- Lemon slices for garnish (optional)

Instructions:

1. Place each chicken breast between two sheets of plastic wrap. Use a meat mallet or rolling pin to pound the chicken to an even thickness, about 1/4 inch.
2. Season both sides of the chicken breasts with salt and pepper.
3. In a shallow dish, combine almond flour and grated Parmesan cheese.
4. Dredge each chicken breast in the almond flour mixture, shaking off any excess.
5. In a large skillet, heat butter and olive oil over mediumhigh heat.
6. Add the chicken breasts to the skillet and cook until golden brown and cooked through, about 45 minutes per side. Remove from the skillet and set aside.
7. In the same skillet, add minced garlic and cook until fragrant, about 1 minute.
8. Deglaze the skillet with chicken broth, scraping up any browned bits from the bottom of the pan.
9. Stir in fresh lemon juice and capers. Cook for another 2 minutes.
10. Return the chicken breasts to the skillet, spooning the sauce over them.
11. Cook for an additional 23 minutes, allowing the chicken to heat through and the sauce to thicken slightly.
12. Remove from heat and garnish with chopped fresh parsley and lemon slices, if desired.
13. Serve hot and enjoy this classic chicken piccata dish!

Nutritional Info (per serving): Calories: 350 | Fat: 20g | Carbs: 5g | Protein: 35g

Atkins Diet Feature: This chicken piccata recipe uses almond flour instead of traditional flour, making it low in carbs and suitable for the Atkins Diet. It's a light and tangy dish that's perfect for a weeknight dinner or a special occasion!

Prep: 15 mins | Cook: 20 mins | Serves: 4

Ingredients:
- 1 lb chicken tenders (about 450g)
- 1 cup almond flour (100g)
- 1/2 cup grated Parmesan cheese (50g)
- 1 teaspoon garlic powder (5g)
- 1 teaspoon paprika (5g)
- 2 large eggs, beaten
- Salt and pepper to taste
- Cooking spray

Instructions:
1. Preheat your oven to 400°F (200°C). Line a baking sheet with parchment paper and lightly coat it with cooking spray.
2. In a shallow dish, combine almond flour, grated Parmesan cheese, garlic powder, paprika, salt, and pepper.
3. Dip each chicken tender in beaten eggs, then dredge in the almond flour mixture, pressing to coat evenly.
4. Place the coated chicken tenders on the prepared baking sheet, leaving space between each piece.
5. Lightly spray the tops of the chicken tenders with cooking spray.
6. Bake in the preheated oven for 1820 minutes, or until the chicken is golden brown and cooked through, flipping halfway through cooking.
7. Remove from the oven and let them cool slightly before serving.
8. Serve hot and enjoy these crispy baked chicken tenders with your favorite dipping sauce!

Nutritional Info (per serving): Calories: 300 | Fat: 15g | Carbs: 5g | Protein: 35g

Atkins Diet Feature: These crispy baked chicken tenders are low in carbs and high in protein, making them a great option for the Atkins Diet. They're crunchy on the outside, tender on the inside, and perfect for dipping into your favorite sauce!

Prep: 15 mins | Cook: 25 mins | Serves: 4

Ingredients:
- 4 boneless, skinless chicken breasts (about 600g)
- Salt and pepper to taste
- 2 tablespoons olive oil (30ml)
- 2 cloves garlic, minced (2 cloves)
- 4 cups fresh spinach leaves (120g)
- 1/2 cup heavy cream (120ml)
- 1/4 cup grated Parmesan cheese (25g)
- 1/4 cup shredded mozzarella cheese (25g)
- 1/4 teaspoon red pepper flakes (1g)
- Lemon wedges for serving (optional)

Instructions:
1. Season both sides of the chicken breasts with salt and pepper.
2. In a large skillet, heat olive oil over mediumhigh heat.
3. Add the seasoned chicken breasts to the skillet and cook until golden brown on both sides and cooked through, about 45 minutes per side. Remove from the skillet and set aside.
4. In the same skillet, add minced garlic and cook until fragrant, about 1 minute.
5. Add fresh spinach leaves to the skillet and cook until wilted, about 23 minutes.
6. Stir in heavy cream, grated Parmesan cheese, shredded mozzarella cheese, and red pepper flakes. Cook until the sauce thickens slightly, about 23 minutes.
7. Return the cooked chicken breasts to the skillet, spooning the sauce over them.
8. Cook for an additional 23 minutes, allowing the chicken to heat through and the flavors to meld.
9. Remove from heat and squeeze lemon juice over the chicken if desired.
10.   Serve hot and enjoy this creamy and flavorful chicken Florentine!

Nutritional Info (per serving): Calories: 380 | Fat: 20g | Carbs: 5g | Protein: 40g

Atkins Diet Feature: This chicken Florentine recipe is low in carbs and high in protein, making it suitable for the Atkins Diet. It's a rich and satisfying dish that's perfect for a cozy dinner at home!

Turkey Meatloaf

Prep: 15 mins | Cook: 1 hour | Serves: 6

Ingredients:
- 1 lb ground turkey (about 450g)
- 1/2 cup almond flour (50g)
- 1/4 cup grated Parmesan cheese (25g)
- 1/4 cup sugarfree ketchup (60ml)
- 1/4 cup chopped onion (1/4 onion)
- 1/4 cup chopped bell pepper (1/4 pepper)
- 1 large egg
- 2 cloves garlic, minced (2 cloves)
- 1 teaspoon dried oregano (5g)
- 1 teaspoon dried thyme (5g)
- 1 teaspoon garlic powder (5g)
- Salt and pepper to taste

Instructions:
1. Preheat your oven to 375°F (190°C). Grease a loaf pan with olive oil or nonstick cooking spray.
2. In a large mixing bowl, combine ground turkey, almond flour, grated Parmesan cheese, sugarfree ketchup, chopped onion, chopped bell pepper, minced garlic, dried oregano, dried thyme, garlic powder, salt, and pepper.
3. Mix until all ingredients are well combined.
4. Transfer the turkey mixture into the prepared loaf pan, pressing it down evenly.
5. Bake in the preheated oven for 5060 minutes, or until the meatloaf is cooked through and the top is golden brown.
6. Remove from the oven and let it rest for a few minutes before slicing.
7. Serve slices of turkey meatloaf hot, and enjoy this comforting and flavorful dish!

Nutritional Info (per serving): Calories: 250 | Fat: 12g | Carbs: 5g | Protein: 25g

Atkins Diet Feature: This turkey meatloaf is low in carbs and high in protein, making it a perfect option for the Atkins Diet. It's a healthier twist on a classic comfort food that's sure to satisfy your cravings!

Turkey Sausage Stuffed Peppers

Prep: 15 mins | Cook: 40 mins | Serves: 4

Ingredients:
- 4 large bell peppers, halved and seeds removed
- 1 lb turkey sausage
- 1 cup cauliflower rice (100g)
- 1/2 cup shredded mozzarella cheese (50g)
- 1/4 cup chopped onion (1/4 onion)
- 2 cloves garlic, minced (2 cloves)
- 1 teaspoon Italian seasoning (5g)
- Salt and pepper to taste
- Chopped fresh parsley for garnish (optional)

Instructions:
1. Preheat your oven to 375°F (190°C). Grease a baking dish with olive oil or nonstick cooking spray.
2. Place the halved bell peppers in the prepared baking dish, cut side up.
3. In a skillet, cook the turkey sausage over medium heat until browned and cooked through, breaking it apart with a spoon as it cooks.
4. Add chopped onion and minced garlic to the skillet with the turkey sausage. Cook until the onion is softened and translucent, about 34 minutes.
5. Stir in cauliflower rice, Italian seasoning, salt, and pepper. Cook for another 23 minutes, until the cauliflower rice is tender.
6. Remove the skillet from heat and stir in shredded mozzarella cheese until melted and well combined.
7. Spoon the turkey sausage mixture into each bell pepper half, filling them evenly.

8. Cover the baking dish with foil and bake in the preheated oven for 2530 minutes, or until the peppers are tender.
9. Remove the foil and bake for an additional 510 minutes, or until the cheese is bubbly and golden brown.
10.   Remove from the oven and let them cool slightly before serving.
11.   Garnish with chopped fresh parsley if desired.
12.   Serve hot and enjoy these delicious and satisfying turkey sausage stuffed peppers!

Nutritional Info (per serving): Calories: 300 | Fat: 15g | Carbs: 10g | Protein: 25g

Atkins Diet Feature: These turkey sausage stuffed peppers are low in carbs and high in protein, making them a great option for the Atkins Diet. They're packed with savory flavors and make a nutritious and filling meal!

Turkey Burgers

Prep: 10 mins | Cook: 10 mins | Serves: 4

Ingredients:
- 1 lb ground turkey (about 450g)
- 1/4 cup almond flour (25g)
- 1/4 cup grated Parmesan cheese (25g)
- 2 tablespoons chopped fresh parsley
- 1 teaspoon garlic powder (5g)
- 1 teaspoon onion powder (5g)
- Salt and pepper to taste
- Lettuce leaves, tomato slices, and onion slices for serving

Instructions:
1. In a large mixing bowl, combine ground turkey, almond flour, grated Parmesan cheese, chopped fresh parsley, garlic powder, onion powder, salt, and pepper.
2. Mix until all ingredients are well combined.
3. Divide the turkey mixture into 4 equal portions and shape them into burger patties.

4. Preheat your grill or grill pan over mediumhigh heat.
5. Cook the turkey burgers for 45 minutes on each side, or until they are cooked through and reach an internal temperature of 165°F (75°C).
6. Remove the turkey burgers from the grill and let them rest for a few minutes.
7. Serve the turkey burgers on lettuce leaves with tomato slices and onion slices.
8. Enjoy these juicy and flavorful turkey burgers as a delicious and healthy meal!

Nutritional Info (per serving, without toppings): Calories: 250 | Fat: 15g | Carbs: 3g | Protein: 25g

Atkins Diet Feature: These turkey burgers are low in carbs and high in protein, making them a perfect option for the Atkins Diet. They're easy to make and customizable with your favorite toppings, making them a great choice for a quick and satisfying meal!

CHAPTER SIX: BEEF, PORK AND LAMB MAIN DISHES RECIPES

Classic Meatloaf

Prep: 15 mins | Cook: 1 hour | Serves: 6

Ingredients:
- 1 lb ground beef (about 450g)
- 1/2 cup almond flour (50g)
- 1/4 cup grated Parmesan cheese (25g)
- 1/4 cup sugarfree ketchup (60ml)
- 1/4 cup diced onion (1/4 onion)
- 1/4 cup diced bell pepper (1/4 pepper)
- 2 cloves garlic, minced (2 cloves)
- 1 large egg
- 1 teaspoon Worcestershire sauce (5ml)
- Salt and pepper to taste

Instructions:
1. Preheat your oven to 350°F (175°C). Grease a loaf pan with olive oil or nonstick cooking spray.
2. In a large mixing bowl, combine ground beef, almond flour, grated Parmesan cheese, sugarfree ketchup, diced onion, diced bell pepper, minced garlic, egg, Worcestershire sauce, salt, and pepper.
3. Mix the ingredients thoroughly, but avoid overmixing to keep the meatloaf tender.
4. Transfer the mixture into the prepared loaf pan, pressing it down evenly.
5. Bake in the preheated oven for 5060 minutes, or until the meatloaf is cooked through and the top is browned.
6. Remove from the oven and let it rest for a few minutes before slicing.
7. Serve slices of meatloaf hot, and enjoy this comforting and flavorful dish!

Nutritional Info (per serving): Calories: 300 | Fat: 20g | Carbs: 5g | Protein: 25g

Atkins Diet Feature: This classic meatloaf recipe is low in carbs and high in protein, making it perfect for the Atkins Diet. It's a hearty and satisfying dish that's easy to make and great for leftovers!

Stuffed Peppers

Prep: 20 mins | Cook: 40 mins | Serves: 4

Ingredients:
- 4 large bell peppers, halved and seeds removed
- 1 lb ground pork (about 450g)
- 1 cup cauliflower rice (100g)
- 1/2 cup shredded cheddar cheese (50g)
- 1/4 cup diced onion (1/4 onion)
- 2 cloves garlic, minced (2 cloves)
- 1 teaspoon Italian seasoning (5g)
- Salt and pepper to taste
- Chopped fresh parsley for garnish (optional)

Instructions:
1. Preheat your oven to 375°F (190°C). Grease a baking dish with olive oil or nonstick cooking spray.
2. Place the halved bell peppers in the prepared baking dish, cut side up.
3. In a skillet, cook the ground pork over medium heat until browned and cooked through, breaking it apart with a spoon as it cooks.
4. Add diced onion and minced garlic to the skillet with the ground pork. Cook until the onion is softened and translucent, about 34 minutes.
5. Stir in cauliflower rice, Italian seasoning, salt, and pepper. Cook for another 23 minutes, until the cauliflower rice is tender.
6. Remove the skillet from heat and stir in shredded cheddar cheese until melted and well combined.
7. Spoon the pork and cauliflower rice mixture into each bell pepper half, filling them evenly.
8. Cover the baking dish with foil and bake in the preheated oven for 2530 minutes, or until the peppers are tender.
9. Remove the foil and bake for an additional 510 minutes, or until the cheese is bubbly and golden brown.
10. Remove from the oven and let them cool slightly before serving.
11. Garnish with chopped fresh parsley if desired.

12.   Serve hot and enjoy these delicious and satisfying stuffed peppers!

Nutritional Info (per serving): Calories: 350 | Fat: 20g | Carbs: 10g | Protein: 25g

Atkins Diet Feature: These stuffed peppers are low in carbs and high in protein, making them a great option for the Atkins Diet. They're packed with savory flavors and make a nutritious and filling meal!

Pot Roast

Prep: 15 mins | Cook: 3 hours | Serves: 6

Ingredients:
- 3 lbs beef chuck roast (about 1.4kg)
- 2 tablespoons olive oil (30ml)
- 1 onion, sliced
- 3 cloves garlic, minced (3 cloves)
- 2 cups beef broth (480ml)
- 1 cup diced tomatoes (240g)
- 1 cup sliced carrots (150g)
- 1 cup sliced celery (120g)
- 2 teaspoons dried thyme (10g)
- 2 teaspoons dried rosemary (10g)
- Salt and pepper to taste

Instructions:
1. Preheat your oven to 325°F (160°C).
2. Season the beef chuck roast generously with salt and pepper.
3. In a large Dutch oven or ovensafe pot, heat olive oil over mediumhigh heat.
4. Add the seasoned beef chuck roast to the pot and sear on all sides until browned, about 45 minutes per side. Remove from the pot and set aside.
5. Add sliced onion to the pot and cook until softened, about 34 minutes.
6. Stir in minced garlic and cook until fragrant, about 1 minute.

7. Return the seared beef chuck roast to the pot.
8. Pour beef broth and diced tomatoes over the roast.
9. Add sliced carrots, sliced celery, dried thyme, and dried rosemary to the pot.
10. Cover the pot with a lid and transfer it to the preheated oven.
11. Cook for 2 1/2 to 3 hours, or until the beef is tender and falls apart easily with a fork.
12. Remove the pot roast from the oven and let it rest for a few minutes before serving.
13. Slice the pot roast against the grain and serve with the vegetables and juices from the pot.
14. Enjoy this hearty and comforting pot roast as a delicious meal!

Nutritional Info (per serving): Calories: 400 | Fat: 25g | Carbs: 5g | Protein: 35g

Atkins Diet Feature: This pot roast recipe is low in carbs and high in protein, making it suitable for the Atkins Diet. It's a classic comfort food dish that's perfect for a cozy dinner with family or friends!

Steak Fajitas

Prep: 15 mins | Cook: 15 mins | Serves: 4

Ingredients:
- 1 lb flank steak (about 450g), thinly sliced
- 1 tablespoon olive oil (15ml)
- 1 onion, sliced
- 1 bell pepper, sliced
- 2 cloves garlic, minced (2 cloves)
- 1 tablespoon chili powder (5g)
- 1 teaspoon ground cumin (5g)
- 1 teaspoon paprika (5g)
- Salt and pepper to taste
- Juice of 1 lime
- Tortillas, lettuce, shredded cheese, salsa, sour cream, and guacamole for serving

1. In a bowl, combine the sliced flank steak with chili powder, ground cumin, paprika, salt, pepper, and the juice of half a lime. Allow to marinate for at least 10 minutes.
2. Heat olive oil in a large skillet over mediumhigh heat.
3. Add the sliced onion and bell pepper to the skillet and cook until softened, about 5 minutes.
4. Add minced garlic to the skillet and cook for an additional minute until fragrant.
5. Push the vegetables to one side of the skillet and add the marinated flank steak to the other side.
6. Cook the steak for 34 minutes, stirring occasionally, until browned and cooked to your desired level of doneness.
7. Combine the steak with the vegetables in the skillet and squeeze the juice of the remaining lime over the mixture.
8. Serve the steak fajitas hot with tortillas, lettuce, shredded cheese, salsa, sour cream, and guacamole.
9. Enjoy assembling your own delicious steak fajitas!

Nutritional Info (per serving, without tortillas and toppings): Calories: 250 | Fat: 12g | Carbs: 5g | Protein: 30g

Atkins Diet Feature: These steak fajitas are low in carbs and high in protein, making them suitable for the Atkins Diet. They're packed with flavor and perfect for a quick and satisfying weeknight dinner!

Bacon Cheeseburger Casserole

Prep: 20 mins | Cook: 30 mins | Serves: 6

Ingredients:

- 1 lb ground beef (about 450g)
- 6 slices bacon, cooked and crumbled
- 1 onion, diced
- 2 cloves garlic, minced (2 cloves)
- 1 cup diced tomatoes (240g)

- 1 cup shredded cheddar cheese (100g)
- 1/2 cup sugarfree ketchup (120ml)
- 1/4 cup mayonnaise (60ml)
- 1 tablespoon mustard (15ml)
- Salt and pepper to taste
- Chopped lettuce, diced tomatoes, and pickles for serving

Instructions:

1. Preheat your oven to 350°F (175°C). Grease a casserole dish with olive oil or nonstick cooking spray.
2. In a skillet, cook the ground beef over medium heat until browned and cooked through. Drain excess fat if needed.
3. Add diced onion and minced garlic to the skillet with the ground beef. Cook until the onion is softened and translucent, about 34 minutes.
4. In a bowl, combine the cooked ground beef mixture with diced tomatoes and crumbled bacon. Season with salt and pepper to taste.
5. Spread the beef mixture evenly in the prepared casserole dish.
6. In another bowl, mix together sugarfree ketchup, mayonnaise, and mustard until well combined.
7. Spread the ketchup mixture over the beef mixture in the casserole dish.
8. Top with shredded cheddar cheese.
9. Bake in the preheated oven for 2530 minutes, or until the cheese is melted and bubbly.
10. Remove from the oven and let it cool for a few minutes before serving.
11. Serve the bacon cheeseburger casserole hot with chopped lettuce, diced tomatoes, and pickles.
12. Enjoy this delicious and satisfying casserole with all the flavors of a classic bacon cheeseburger!

Nutritional Info (per serving): Calories: 400 | Fat: 25g | Carbs: 5g | Protein: 35g

Atkins Diet Feature: This bacon cheeseburger casserole is low in carbs and high in protein, making it a perfect option for the Atkins Diet. It's a familyfriendly dish that's sure to be a hit with everyone at the dinner table!

Prep: 30 mins | Cook: 1 hour | Serves: 8

Ingredients:
- 1 lb ground pork (about 450g)
- 1 onion, diced
- 2 cloves garlic, minced (2 cloves)
- 1 cup diced tomatoes (240g)
- 1 cup tomato sauce (240ml)
- 1 tablespoon tomato paste (15g)
- 1 tablespoon Italian seasoning (5g)
- Salt and pepper to taste
- 2 medium zucchinis, thinly sliced lengthwise
- 2 cups shredded mozzarella cheese (200g)
- 1/4 cup grated Parmesan cheese (25g)
- Chopped fresh basil for garnish (optional)

Instructions:
1. Preheat your oven to 375°F (190°C). Grease a casserole dish with olive oil or nonstick cooking spray.
2. In a skillet, cook the ground pork over medium heat until browned and cooked through. Drain excess fat if needed.
3. Add diced onion and minced garlic to the skillet with the ground pork. Cook until the onion is softened and translucent, about 34 minutes.
4. Stir in diced tomatoes, tomato sauce, tomato paste, Italian seasoning, salt, and pepper. Simmer for 1015 minutes, allowing the flavors to meld.
5. Arrange a layer of thinly sliced zucchini in the bottom of the prepared casserole dish.
6. Spread a layer of the pork and tomato sauce mixture over the zucchini.
7. Sprinkle a layer of shredded mozzarella cheese over the pork mixture.
8. Repeat the layers until all ingredients are used, finishing with a layer of mozzarella cheese on top.
9. Sprinkle grated Parmesan cheese over the top layer.
10. Cover the casserole dish with foil and bake in the preheated oven for 30 minutes.
11. Remove the foil and bake for an additional 1520 minutes, or until the cheese is golden and bubbly.
12. Remove from the oven and let it cool for a few minutes before serving.
13. Garnish with chopped fresh basil if desired.

14.   Serve the lasagna hot and enjoy this lowcarb twist on a classic Italian favorite!

Nutritional Info (per serving): Calories: 350 | Fat: 20g | Carbs: 10g | Protein: 30g

Atkins Diet Feature: This lasagna recipe replaces traditional pasta with thinly sliced zucchini, making it low in carbs and suitable for the Atkins Diet. It's a comforting and indulgent dish that's perfect for satisfying your Italian food cravings while sticking to your lowcarb lifestyle!

Stuffed Cabbage Rolls

Prep: 30 mins | Cook: 1 hour | Serves: 6

Ingredients:
- 1 large head of cabbage
- 1 lb ground beef (about 450g)
- 1 onion, finely chopped
- 2 cloves garlic, minced (2 cloves)
- 1 cup cauliflower rice (100g)
- 1 cup diced tomatoes (240g)
- 1 teaspoon paprika (5g)
- Salt and pepper to taste
- 1 cup beef broth (240ml)
- Chopped fresh parsley for garnish (optional)

Instructions:
1. Preheat your oven to 350°F (175°C).
2. Bring a large pot of salted water to a boil. Carefully remove the core from the cabbage and immerse the whole head in the boiling water. Cook for 57 minutes, or until the outer leaves are soft and pliable. Remove the cabbage from the water and set aside to cool.
3. In a skillet, cook the ground beef over medium heat until browned and cooked through. Drain excess fat if needed.
4. Add finely chopped onion and minced garlic to the skillet with the ground beef. Cook until the onion is softened and translucent, about 34 minutes.

5. Stir in cauliflower rice, diced tomatoes, paprika, salt, and pepper. Cook for another 23 minutes, until the cauliflower rice is tender.
6. Carefully peel off the softened cabbage leaves and lay them flat on a clean surface. Place a spoonful of the beef mixture onto each cabbage leaf and roll them up, tucking in the sides as you go.
7. Place the stuffed cabbage rolls seamside down in a baking dish.
8. Pour beef broth over the cabbage rolls in the baking dish.
9. Cover the baking dish with foil and bake in the preheated oven for 4550 minutes, or until the cabbage rolls are cooked through.
10.   Remove from the oven and let them cool for a few minutes before serving.
11.   Garnish with chopped fresh parsley if desired.
12.   Serve the stuffed cabbage rolls hot and enjoy this comforting and flavorful dish!

Nutritional Info (per serving): Calories: 300 | Fat: 15g | Carbs: 10g | Protein: 25g

Atkins Diet Feature: These stuffed cabbage rolls are low in carbs and high in protein, making them suitable for the Atkins Diet. They're a hearty and satisfying meal that's perfect for cozy dinners or meal prep!

Chili

Prep: 15 mins | Cook: 1 hour | Serves: 6

Ingredients:
- 1 lb ground beef (about 450g)
- 1 onion, diced
- 2 cloves garlic, minced (2 cloves)
- 1 bell pepper, diced
- 1 can (14 oz) diced tomatoes (400g)
- 1 can (14 oz) tomato sauce (400g)
- 1 can (14 oz) kidney beans, drained and rinsed (400g)
- 2 tablespoons chili powder (10g)
- 1 teaspoon ground cumin (5g)
- Salt and pepper to taste
- Shredded cheddar cheese, chopped onions, and sour cream for serving

Instructions:

1. In a large pot or Dutch oven, cook the ground beef over medium heat until browned and cooked through. Drain excess fat if needed.
2. Add diced onion, minced garlic, and diced bell pepper to the pot with the ground beef. Cook until the vegetables are softened, about 57 minutes.
3. Stir in diced tomatoes, tomato sauce, kidney beans, chili powder, ground cumin, salt, and pepper.
4. Bring the chili to a simmer, then reduce the heat to low. Cover and let it simmer for 4560 minutes, stirring occasionally.
5. Adjust seasoning with salt and pepper to taste if needed.
6. Serve the chili hot, garnished with shredded cheddar cheese, chopped onions, and a dollop of sour cream.
7. Enjoy this hearty and flavorful chili as a comforting meal on a chilly day!

Nutritional Info (per serving): Calories: 350 | Fat: 15g | Carbs: 15g | Protein: 25g

Atkins Diet Feature: This chili recipe is relatively low in carbs and high in protein, making it suitable for the Atkins Diet. It's a satisfying and nutritious dish that's perfect for feeding a crowd or for meal prep!

Balsamic Glazed Pork Chops

Prep: 10 mins | Cook: 20 mins | Serves: 4

Ingredients:

- 4 boneless pork chops
- Salt and pepper to taste
- 2 tablespoons olive oil (30ml)
- 1/4 cup balsamic vinegar (60ml)
- 2 tablespoons lowsodium soy sauce (30ml)
- 2 tablespoons honey or sugarfree sweetener (30ml)
- 2 cloves garlic, minced (2 cloves)
- Chopped fresh parsley for garnish (optional)

1. Season both sides of the pork chops with salt and pepper.
2. In a small bowl, whisk together balsamic vinegar, lowsodium soy sauce, honey or sugarfree sweetener, and minced garlic to make the glaze.
3. Heat olive oil in a skillet over mediumhigh heat.
4. Add the pork chops to the skillet and cook for 45 minutes on each side, or until golden brown and cooked through.
5. Reduce the heat to mediumlow and pour the balsamic glaze over the pork chops in the skillet.
6. Cook for an additional 23 minutes, allowing the glaze to thicken and coat the pork chops.
7. Flip the pork chops once more to coat them evenly in the glaze.
8. Remove from the heat and let the pork chops rest for a few minutes.
9. Garnish with chopped fresh parsley if desired.
10. Serve the balsamic glazed pork chops hot, and enjoy the sweet and tangy flavors!

Nutritional Info (per serving): Calories: 300 | Fat: 15g | Carbs: 5g | Protein: 30g

Atkins Diet Feature: These balsamic glazed pork chops are low in carbs and high in protein, making them suitable for the Atkins Diet. They're quick and easy to make, yet full of flavor, making them a great option for busy weeknights!

Sausage and Peppers

Prep: 15 mins | Cook: 25 mins | Serves: 4

Ingredients:
- 1 lb Italian sausage links (about 450g)
- 2 bell peppers, sliced
- 1 onion, sliced
- 2 cloves garlic, minced (2 cloves)
- 1 can (14 oz) diced tomatoes (400g)
- 1 teaspoon Italian seasoning (5g)
- Salt and pepper to taste

- Chopped fresh parsley for garnish (optional)

Instructions:
1. In a large skillet, cook the Italian sausage links over medium heat until browned and cooked through. Remove from the skillet and set aside.
2. In the same skillet, add sliced bell peppers and onion. Cook until softened, about 57 minutes.
3. Add minced garlic to the skillet and cook for an additional minute until fragrant.
4. Slice the cooked Italian sausage links and return them to the skillet.
5. Stir in diced tomatoes (with their juices), Italian seasoning, salt, and pepper.
6. Cook for another 510 minutes, allowing the flavors to meld together.
7. Adjust seasoning with salt and pepper to taste if needed.
8. Garnish with chopped fresh parsley if desired.
9. Serve the sausage and peppers hot, either on their own or over cauliflower rice or zucchini noodles.
10. Enjoy this flavorful and satisfying dish with your favorite lowcarb sides!

Nutritional Info (per serving): Calories: 350 | Fat: 25g | Carbs: 10g | Protein: 20g

Atkins Diet Feature: This sausage and peppers recipe is relatively low in carbs and high in protein, making it suitable for the Atkins Diet. It's a classic combination that's full of savory flavors and perfect for a quick and easy weeknight dinner!

Prep: 20 mins | Cook: 30 mins | Serves: 4

Ingredients:
- 4 large bell peppers, halved and seeds removed
- 1 lb thinly sliced beef steak (about 450g)
- 1 onion, thinly sliced
- 2 cloves garlic, minced (2 cloves)
- 1 cup sliced mushrooms (100g)
- 1 cup shredded provolone cheese (100g)
- Salt and pepper to taste
- Chopped fresh parsley for garnish (optional)

Instructions:
1. Preheat your oven to 375°F (190°C). Grease a baking dish with olive oil or nonstick cooking spray.
2. Place the halved bell peppers in the prepared baking dish, cut side up.
3. In a skillet, cook the thinly sliced beef steak over mediumhigh heat until browned and cooked through. Remove from the skillet and set aside.
4. In the same skillet, add thinly sliced onion and cook until softened and caramelized, about 57 minutes.
5. Add minced garlic and sliced mushrooms to the skillet. Cook until the mushrooms are tender and any liquid has evaporated, about 5 minutes.
6. Return the cooked beef steak to the skillet and mix with the onion and mushroom mixture. Season with salt and pepper to taste.
7. Fill each halved bell pepper with the beef, onion, and mushroom mixture.
8. Top each stuffed pepper with shredded provolone cheese.
9. Cover the baking dish with foil and bake in the preheated oven for 2025 minutes, or until the peppers are tender and the cheese is melted and bubbly.
10. Remove from the oven and let them cool for a few minutes before serving.
11. Garnish with chopped fresh parsley if desired.
12. Serve the Philly cheesesteak stuffed peppers hot and enjoy all the flavors of a classic Philly cheesesteak in a lowcarb, Atkinsfriendly format!

Nutritional Info (per serving): Calories: 300 | Fat: 15g | Carbs: 10g | Protein: 25g

Atkins Diet Feature: These Philly cheesesteak stuffed peppers are low in carbs and high in protein, making them perfect for the Atkins Diet. They're a creative and delicious twist on a beloved sandwich, and they're sure to be a hit with the whole family!

Greek Lamb Burgers

Prep: 15 mins | Cook: 15 mins | Serves: 4

Ingredients:
- 1 lb ground lamb (about 450g)
- 1/4 cup crumbled feta cheese (25g)
- 1/4 cup chopped fresh parsley
- 2 cloves garlic, minced (2 cloves)
- 1 teaspoon dried oregano (5g)
- Salt and pepper to taste
- Lettuce leaves, sliced tomato, sliced cucumber, and tzatziki sauce for serving

Instructions:
1. In a mixing bowl, combine ground lamb, crumbled feta cheese, chopped fresh parsley, minced garlic, dried oregano, salt, and pepper.
2. Mix the ingredients together until well combined, but avoid overmixing to keep the burgers tender.
3. Divide the mixture into 4 equal portions and shape each portion into a burger patty.
4. Heat a grill or grill pan over mediumhigh heat. Grill the lamb burgers for 57 minutes on each side, or until cooked to your desired level of doneness.
5. Remove the burgers from the grill and let them rest for a few minutes.
6. Serve the Greek lamb burgers on lettuce leaves, topped with sliced tomato, sliced cucumber, and a dollop of tzatziki sauce.
7. Enjoy these flavorful and juicy burgers with all the fresh flavors of Greece!

Nutritional Info (per serving): Calories: 350 | Fat: 25g | Carbs: 1g | Protein: 30g

Atkins Diet Feature: These Greek lamb burgers are low in carbs and high in protein, making them suitable for the Atkins Diet. They're bursting with Mediterranean flavors and are perfect for a summer barbecue or a quick weeknight dinner!

Pork Chops in Mushroom Gravy

Prep: 10 mins | Cook: 25 mins | Serves: 4

Ingredients:
- 4 bonein pork chops
- Salt and pepper to taste
- 2 tablespoons olive oil (30ml)
- 1 onion, sliced
- 8 oz mushrooms, sliced (225g)
- 2 cloves garlic, minced (2 cloves)
- 1 cup beef broth (240ml)
- 1/2 cup heavy cream (120ml)
- 1 tablespoon Worcestershire sauce (15ml)
- 1 teaspoon dried thyme (5g)
- Chopped fresh parsley for garnish (optional)

Instructions:
1. Season both sides of the pork chops with salt and pepper.
2. In a large skillet, heat olive oil over mediumhigh heat.
3. Add the pork chops to the skillet and 4. Cook the pork chops for 45 minutes on each side, or until they are browned and cooked through. Remove them from the skillet and set aside.
4. In the same skillet, add sliced onion and mushrooms. Cook until they are softened and browned, about 57 minutes.
5. Add minced garlic to the skillet and cook for an additional minute until fragrant.
6. Pour beef broth into the skillet, scraping the bottom to deglaze and pick up any browned bits.
7. Stir in heavy cream, Worcestershire sauce, and dried thyme. Bring the mixture to a simmer.
8. Return the pork chops to the skillet and spoon some of the mushroom gravy over them.

9. Let the pork chops simmer in the gravy for 57 minutes, allowing the flavors to meld together and the sauce to thicken slightly.
10.   Adjust seasoning with salt and pepper to taste if needed.
11.   Garnish with chopped fresh parsley if desired.
12.   Serve the pork chops hot, spooning mushroom gravy over them.
13.   Enjoy these tender and flavorful pork chops in a rich and creamy mushroom gravy!

Nutritional Info (per serving): Calories: 400 | Fat: 30g | Carbs: 5g | Protein: 25g

Atkins Diet Feature: These pork chops in mushroom gravy are low in carbs and high in protein, making them suitable for the Atkins Diet. The creamy mushroom gravy adds richness and flavor to the tender pork chops, making this dish a comforting and satisfying meal option.

Cajun Shrimp and Sausage Skillet

Prep: 10 mins | Cook: 20 mins | Serves: 4

Ingredients:
- 1 lb large shrimp, peeled and deveined (about 450g)
- 12 oz Andouille sausage, sliced (340g)
- 1 onion, diced
- 1 bell pepper, diced
- 2 cloves garlic, minced (2 cloves)
- 1 teaspoon Cajun seasoning (5g)
- 1/2 teaspoon paprika (2.5g)
- Salt and pepper to taste
- 2 tablespoons olive oil (30ml)
- Chopped fresh parsley for garnish (optional)

Instructions:
1. In a large skillet, heat olive oil over mediumhigh heat.
2. Add sliced Andouille sausage to the skillet and cook until browned, about 5 minutes.

3. Add diced onion and bell pepper to the skillet. Cook until they are softened, about 57 minutes.
4. Add minced garlic to the skillet and cook for an additional minute until fragrant.
5. Season the shrimp with Cajun seasoning, paprika, salt, and pepper.
6. Push the sausage, onion, and bell pepper to the side of the skillet and add the seasoned shrimp to the other side.
7. Cook the shrimp for 23 minutes on each side, or until they are pink and cooked through.
8. Stir everything together in the skillet, mixing the shrimp with the sausage, onion, and bell pepper.
9. Adjust seasoning with salt and pepper to taste if needed.
10. Garnish with chopped fresh parsley if desired.
11. Serve the Cajun shrimp and sausage hot, and enjoy this flavorful and spicy skillet dish!

Nutritional Info (per serving): Calories: 350 | Fat: 20g | Carbs: 5g | Protein: 30g

Atkins Diet Feature: This Cajun shrimp and sausage skillet is low in carbs and high in protein, making it suitable for the Atkins Diet. It's a quick and easy onepan meal that's bursting with bold flavors and perfect for busy weeknights!

Zucchini Lasagna

Prep: 20 mins | Cook: 1 hour | Serves: 6

Ingredients:
- 3 large zucchinis, thinly sliced lengthwise
- 1 lb ground beef (about 450g)
- 1 onion, diced
- 2 cloves garlic, minced (2 cloves)
- 1 can (14 oz) diced tomatoes (400g)
- 1 can (14 oz) tomato sauce (400g)
- 1 tablespoon Italian seasoning (5g)
- Salt and pepper to taste
- 2 cups shredded mozzarella cheese (200g)
- 1/4 cup grated Parmesan cheese (25g)

- Chopped fresh basil for garnish (optional)

Instructions:
1. Preheat your oven to 375°F (190°C). Grease a casserole dish with olive oil or nonstick cooking spray.
2. Place a layer of thinly sliced zucchini in the bottom of the prepared casserole dish.
3. In a skillet, cook the ground beef over medium heat until browned and cooked through. Drain excess fat if needed.
4. Add diced onion and minced garlic to the skillet with the ground beef. Cook until the onion is softened and translucent, about 34 minutes.
5. Stir in diced tomatoes, tomato sauce, Italian seasoning, salt, and pepper. Simmer for 1015 minutes, allowing the flavors to meld.
6. Spread a layer of the meat sauce over the layer of zucchini in the casserole dish.
7. Sprinkle a layer of shredded mozzarella cheese over the meat sauce.
8. Repeat the layers until all ingredients are used, finishing with a layer of mozzarella cheese on top.
9. Sprinkle grated Parmesan cheese over the top layer.
10. Cover the casserole dish with foil and bake in the preheated oven for 30 minutes.
11. Remove the foil and bake for an additional 1520 minutes, or until the cheese is melted and bubbly.
12. Remove from the oven and let it cool for a few minutes before serving.
13. Garnish with chopped fresh basil if desired.
14. Serve the zucchini lasagna hot, and enjoy this lowcarb twist on a classic Italian favorite!

Nutritional Info (per serving): Calories: 300 | Fat: 15g | Carbs: 10g | Protein: 25g

Atkins Diet Feature: This zucchini lasagna recipe replaces traditional pasta with thinly sliced zucchini, making it low in carbs and suitable for the Atkins Diet. It's a comforting and indulgent dish that's perfect for anyone looking to cut down on carbs while still enjoying their favorite comfort foods!

Lemon Garlic Shrimp

Prep: 10 mins | Cook: 10 mins | Serves: 4

Ingredients:
- 1 lb large shrimp, peeled and deveined (about 450g)
- 4 cloves garlic, minced
- Zest and juice of 1 lemon
- 2 tablespoons olive oil (30ml)
- Salt and pepper to taste
- Chopped fresh parsley for garnish (optional)

Instructions:
1. In a bowl, toss the shrimp with minced garlic, lemon zest, lemon juice, olive oil, salt, and pepper.
2. Heat a skillet over mediumhigh heat.
3. Add the seasoned shrimp to the skillet and cook for 23 minutes on each side, or until they are pink and cooked through.
4. Garnish with chopped fresh parsley if desired.
5. Serve the lemon garlic shrimp hot, and enjoy the bright and zesty flavors!

Nutritional Info (per serving): Calories: 200 | Fat: 8g | Carbs: 3g | Protein: 25g

Atkins Diet Feature: This lemon garlic shrimp recipe is low in carbs and high in protein, making it suitable for the Atkins Diet. It's a quick and flavorful seafood dish that's perfect for busy weeknights!

Cajun Shrimp

Prep: 10 mins | Cook: 10 mins | Serves: 4

Ingredients:

- 1 lb large shrimp, peeled and deveined (about 450g)
- 2 tablespoons Cajun seasoning (10g)
- 2 tablespoons olive oil (30ml)
- Salt to taste
- Lemon wedges for serving

Instructions:

1. In a bowl, toss the shrimp with Cajun seasoning and olive oil until evenly coated.
2. Heat a skillet over mediumhigh heat.
3. Add the seasoned shrimp to the skillet and cook for 23 minutes on each side, or until they are pink and cooked through.
4. Season with salt to taste.
5. Serve the Cajun shrimp hot, with lemon wedges on the side.
6. Enjoy the spicy and flavorful Cajun seasoning with the juicy shrimp!

Nutritional Info (per serving): Calories: 220 | Fat: 10g | Carbs: 2g | Protein: 30g

Atkins Diet Feature: These Cajun shrimp are low in carbs and high in protein, making them suitable for the Atkins Diet. They're packed with bold and spicy flavors that will satisfy your cravings!

Bacon Wrapped Scallops

Prep: 15 mins | Cook: 15 mins | Serves: 4

Ingredients:
- 12 large scallops
- 6 slices bacon
- Salt and pepper to taste
- Toothpicks

Instructions:
1. Preheat your oven to 400°F (200°C).
2. Season the scallops with salt and pepper.
3. Cut each slice of bacon in half crosswise.
4. Wrap each scallop with a half slice of bacon and secure with a toothpick.
5. Place the baconwrapped scallops on a baking sheet lined with parchment paper.
6. Bake in the preheated oven for 1215 minutes, or until the bacon is crispy and the scallops are cooked through.
7. Remove from the oven and let them cool for a few minutes.
8. Serve the baconwrapped scallops hot, and enjoy the indulgent combination of savory bacon and sweet scallops!

Nutritional Info (per serving): Calories: 250 | Fat: 15g | Carbs: 2g | Protein: 25g

Atkins Diet Feature: These baconwrapped scallops are low in carbs and high in protein, making them suitable for the Atkins Diet. They're an elegant and delicious appetizer or main dish that's sure to impress!

Baked Salmon

Prep: 10 mins | Cook: 20 mins | Serves: 4

Ingredients:
- 4 salmon fillets
- 2 tablespoons olive oil (30ml)
- 2 cloves garlic, minced
- 1 teaspoon dried dill (5g)
- Salt and pepper to taste
- Lemon wedges for serving

Instructions:
1. Preheat your oven to 375°F (190°C). Line a baking sheet with parchment paper.
2. Place the salmon fillets on the prepared baking sheet.
3. In a small bowl, mix together olive oil, minced garlic, dried dill, salt, and pepper.
4. Brush the olive oil mixture over the salmon fillets, coating them evenly.
5. Bake in the preheated oven for 1520 minutes, or until the salmon is cooked through and flakes easily with a fork.
6. Remove from the oven and let them cool for a few minutes.
7. Serve the baked salmon hot, with lemon wedges on the side.
8. Enjoy the tender and flavorful baked salmon as a healthy and satisfying meal!

Nutritional Info (per serving): Calories: 300 | Fat: 15g | Carbs: 1g | Protein: 30g

Atkins Diet Feature: This baked salmon recipe is low in carbs and high in protein, making it suitable for the Atkins Diet. It's a simple yet delicious way to enjoy the natural flavors of salmon!

Tuna Casserole

Prep: 15 mins | Cook: 30 mins | Serves: 6

Ingredients:
- 8 oz lowcarb pasta, cooked according to package instructions (225g)
- 2 cans (5 oz each) tuna, drained (140g each)
- 1 cup diced celery (100g)
- 1 cup diced bell pepper (100g)
- 1 cup diced onion (100g)
- 1 cup shredded cheddar cheese (100g)
- 1 cup heavy cream (240 ml)
- 1/4 cup grated Parmesan cheese (25g)
- 2 tablespoons unsalted butter (30g)
- 2 cloves garlic, minced
- Salt and pepper to taste
- Chopped fresh parsley for garnish (optional)

Instructions:
1. Preheat your oven to 375°F (190°C). Grease a baking dish with butter or nonstick cooking spray.
2. In a large mixing bowl, combine cooked pasta, drained tuna, diced celery, diced bell pepper, diced onion, shredded cheddar cheese, heavy cream, minced garlic, salt, and pepper. Mix until well combined.
3. Transfer the tuna mixture to the prepared baking dish, spreading it out evenly.
4. Sprinkle grated Parmesan cheese over the top.
5. Cut the unsalted butter into small pieces and scatter them over the top of the casserole.
6. Cover the baking dish with foil and bake in the preheated oven for 20 minutes.
7. Remove the foil and bake for an additional 10 minutes, or until the casserole is bubbly and golden brown on top.
8. Remove from the oven and let it cool for a few minutes.
9. Garnish with chopped fresh parsley if desired.
10. Serve the tuna casserole hot, and enjoy this comforting and hearty dish!

Nutritional Info (per serving): Calories: 350 | Fat: 20g | Carbs: 10g | Protein: 25g

Atkins Diet Feature: This tuna casserole is relatively low in carbs and high in protein, making it suitable for the Atkins Diet. It's a creamy and flavorful dish that's perfect for a cozy dinner at home!

Tuna Melts

Prep: 10 mins | Cook: 10 mins | Serves: 4

Ingredients:
- 4 English muffins, split and toasted
- 2 cans (5 oz each) tuna, drained (140g each)
- 1/4 cup mayonnaise (60ml)
- 1/4 cup diced celery (25g)
- 1/4 cup diced red onion (25g)
- 1/2 cup shredded cheddar cheese (50g)
- 1 tablespoon Dijon mustard (15ml)
- Salt and pepper to taste
- Sliced tomato for topping
- Fresh parsley for garnish (optional)

Instructions:
1. Preheat your oven's broiler.
2. In a mixing bowl, combine drained tuna, mayonnaise, diced celery, diced red onion, shredded cheddar cheese, Dijon mustard, salt, and pepper. Mix until well combined.
3. Place the toasted English muffins on a baking sheet lined with parchment paper.
4. Spread the tuna mixture evenly on top of each English muffin half.
5. Top each tuna melt with a slice of tomato.
6. Place the baking sheet under the broiler and broil for 35 minutes, or until the cheese is melted and bubbly.
7. Remove from the oven and let them cool for a minute.
8. Garnish with fresh parsley if desired.
9. Serve the tuna melts hot, and enjoy this classic and comforting dish!

Nutritional Info (per serving): Calories: 300 | Fat: 15g | Carbs: 20g | Protein: 20g

Atkins Diet Feature: These tuna melts can be enjoyed in moderation on the Atkins Diet. While they are higher in carbs due to the English muffins, they provide a good source of protein and can be included as part of a balanced meal plan.

Crab Cakes

Prep: 20 mins | Cook: 15 mins | Serves: 4

Ingredients:
- 1 lb lump crab meat (about 450g)
- 1/4 cup almond flour (25g)
- 1/4 cup mayonnaise (60ml)
- 1 large egg
- 2 tablespoons chopped fresh parsley
- 1 tablespoon Dijon mustard (15ml)
- 1 teaspoon Old Bay seasoning (5g)
- Salt and pepper to taste
- 2 tablespoons olive oil (30ml)

Instructions:
1. In a mixing bowl, combine lump crab meat, almond flour, mayonnaise, egg, chopped fresh parsley, Dijon mustard, Old Bay seasoning, salt, and pepper. Mix until well combined.
2. Divide the crab mixture into 8 equal portions and shape each portion into a patty.
3. Heat olive oil in a skillet over medium heat.
4. Add the crab cakes to the skillet and cook for 34 minutes on each side, or until they are golden brown and heated through.
5. Remove from the skillet and let them cool for a minute.
6. Serve the crab cakes hot, and enjoy the crispy exterior and tender crab meat inside!

Nutritional Info (per serving): Calories: 250 | Fat: 15g | Carbs: 5g | Protein: 20g

Atkins Diet Feature: These crab cakes are low in carbs and high in protein, making them suitable for the Atkins Diet. They're packed with delicious crab flavor and make a delightful appetizer or main course!

Shrimp Scampi Zoodles

Prep: 15 mins | Cook: 10 mins | Serves: 4

Ingredients:
- 1 lb large shrimp, peeled and deveined (about 450g)
- 4 medium zucchinis, spiralized into noodles
- 4 cloves garlic, minced
- 1/4 cup unsalted butter (60g)
- 1/4 cup dry white wine (60ml)
- Juice of 1 lemon
- Salt and pepper to taste
- Chopped fresh parsley for garnish (optional)

Instructions:
1. Heat unsalted butter in a large skillet over medium heat.
2. Add minced garlic to the skillet and cook for 1 minute until fragrant.
3. Add the spiralized zucchini noodles to the skillet and toss to coat them in the garlic butter.
4. Cook the zoodles for 23 minutes, stirring occasionally, until they are just tender. Remove them from the skillet and set aside.
5. In the same skillet, add dry white wine and lemon juice. Bring the mixture to a simmer.
6. Add the peeled and deveined shrimp to the skillet and cook for 23 minutes, or until they are pink and cooked through.
7. Season with salt and pepper to taste.
8. Return the cooked zucchini noodles to the skillet and toss with the shrimp and sauce until everything is well combined.
9. Remove from heat and garnish with chopped fresh parsley if desired.
10. Serve the shrimp scampi zoodles hot, and enjoy this light and flavorful dish!

Nutritional Info (per serving): Calories: 220 | Fat: 10g | Carbs: 5g | Protein: 25g

Atkins Diet Feature: This shrimp scampi zoodles recipe is low in carbs and high in protein, making it suitable for the Atkins Diet. It's a healthy and delicious alternative to traditional pasta dishes!

Clams Casino

Prep: 15 mins | Cook: 10 mins | Serves: 4

Ingredients:
- 24 fresh clams, scrubbed and cleaned
- 4 slices bacon, diced
- 1/4 cup diced red bell pepper (25g)
- 1/4 cup diced green bell pepper (25g)
- 2 cloves garlic, minced
- 1/4 cup grated Parmesan cheese (25g)
- 2 tablespoons chopped fresh parsley
- Salt and pepper to taste
- Lemon wedges for serving

Instructions:
1. Preheat your oven's broiler.
2. In a skillet, cook diced bacon over medium heat until crispy. Remove from the skillet and set aside, leaving the bacon grease in the skillet.
3. In the same skillet with bacon grease, add diced red bell pepper, diced green bell pepper, and minced garlic. Cook for 23 minutes until softened.
4. Remove the skillet from heat and stir in cooked bacon, grated Parmesan cheese, chopped fresh parsley, salt, and pepper.
5. Place the cleaned clams on a baking sheet lined with foil.
6. Spoon the bacon mixture onto each clam, dividing it evenly among them.
7. Place the baking sheet under the broiler and broil for 57 minutes, or until the clams are cooked through and the topping is golden brown and bubbly.
8. Remove from the oven and let them cool for a minute.
9. Serve the clams casino hot, with lemon wedges on the side.
10.   Enjoy these delicious and savory clams as a delightful appetizer or main course!

Nutritional Info (per serving): Calories: 180 | Fat: 10g | Carbs: 5g | Protein: 15g

Atkins Diet Feature: These clams casino are low in carbs and high in protein, making them suitable for the Atkins Diet. They're a flavorful and elegant seafood dish that's perfect for entertaining or special occasions!

Salmon Cakes

Prep: 15 mins | Cook: 15 mins | Serves: 4

Ingredients:
- 2 cans (14.75 oz each) canned salmon, drained and flaked (about 415g each)
- 1/2 cup almond flour (50g)
- 1/4 cup mayonnaise (60ml)
- 2 green onions, finely chopped
- 1 large egg
- 1 tablespoon Dijon mustard (15ml)
- 1 tablespoon lemon juice (15ml)
- 1 teaspoon Old Bay seasoning (5g)
- Salt and pepper to taste
- 2 tablespoons olive oil (30ml)

Instructions:
1. In a mixing bowl, combine canned salmon, almond flour, mayonnaise, chopped green onions, egg, Dijon mustard, lemon juice, Old Bay seasoning, salt, and pepper. Mix until well combined.
2. Divide the salmon mixture into 8 equal portions and shape each portion into a patty.
3. Heat olive oil in a skillet over medium heat.
4. Add the salmon cakes to the skillet and cook for 34 minutes on each side, or until they are golden brown and heated through.
5. Remove from the skillet and let them cool for a minute.
6. Serve the salmon cakes hot, and enjoy the crispy exterior and tender salmon inside!

Nutritional Info (per serving): Calories: 250 | Fat: 15g | Carbs: 5g | Protein: 20g

Atkins Diet Feature: These salmon cakes are low in carbs and high in protein, making them suitable for the Atkins Diet. They're a delicious and nutritious way to enjoy the benefits of omega3rich salmon!

Tuna Stuffed Avocado

Prep: 10 mins | Cook: 0 mins | Serves: 2

Ingredients:
- 1 ripe avocado, halved and pitted
- 1 can (5 oz) tuna, drained (140g)
- 2 tablespoons mayonnaise (30ml)
- 1 tablespoon diced red onion (15g)
- 1 tablespoon diced celery (15g)
- 1 tablespoon chopped fresh parsley
- 1 teaspoon lemon juice (5ml)
- Salt and pepper to taste

Instructions:
1. In a mixing bowl, combine drained tuna, mayonnaise, diced red onion, diced celery, chopped fresh parsley, lemon juice, salt, and pepper. Mix until well combined.
2. Scoop out some of the flesh from each avocado half to create a larger cavity for the filling.
3. Spoon the tuna mixture into each avocado half, dividing it evenly among them.
4. Serve the tuna stuffed avocado immediately, and enjoy this simple yet satisfying dish!

Nutritional Info (per serving): Calories: 300 | Fat: 20g | Carbs: 10g | Protein: 20g

Atkins Diet Feature: This tuna stuffed avocado is relatively low in carbs and high in protein, making it suitable for the Atkins Diet. It's a quick and easy meal that's perfect for lunch or a light dinner!

Cajun Fish Tacos

Prep: 15 mins | Cook: 10 mins | Serves: 4

Ingredients:
- 1 lb white fish fillets (such as tilapia or cod)
- 2 tablespoons Cajun seasoning (10g)
- 2 tablespoons olive oil (30ml)
- 8 small lowcarb tortillas
- 1 cup shredded cabbage (100g)
- 1/2 cup diced tomatoes (50g)
- 1/4 cup diced red onion (25g)
- 1/4 cup chopped fresh cilantro
- 1/4 cup sour cream (60ml)
- Lime wedges for serving

Instructions:
1. Season the fish fillets with Cajun seasoning, pressing the seasoning onto both sides.
2. Heat olive oil in a skillet over mediumhigh heat.
3. Add the seasoned fish fillets to the skillet and cook for 34 minutes on each side, or until they are cooked through and flake easily with a fork.
4. Meanwhile, warm the lowcarb tortillas according to the package instructions.
5. To assemble the tacos, place a portion of shredded cabbage on each tortilla.
6. Top with a cooked fish fillet, diced tomatoes, diced red onion, and chopped fresh cilantro.
7. Drizzle with sour cream.
8. Serve the Cajun fish tacos with lime wedges on the side.
9. Enjoy these flavorful and satisfying tacos that are perfect for a quick weeknight dinner or weekend meal!

Nutritional Info (per serving): Calories: 300 | Fat: 15g | Carbs: 15g | Protein: 25g

Atkins Diet Feature: These Cajun fish tacos are relatively low in carbs and high in protein, making them suitable for the Atkins Diet. They're packed with bold flavors and fresh ingredients, making them a delicious and nutritious meal option.

Cod with Garlic Herb Butter

Prep: 10 mins | Cook: 15 mins | Serves: 4

Ingredients:
- 4 cod fillets
- 4 tablespoons unsalted butter (60g)
- 4 cloves garlic, minced
- 2 tablespoons chopped fresh parsley
- 1 tablespoon chopped fresh chives
- 1 teaspoon lemon zest
- Salt and pepper to taste
- Lemon wedges for serving

Instructions:
1. Preheat your oven to 400°F (200°C). Line a baking sheet with parchment paper.
2. Season the cod fillets with salt and pepper on both sides.
3. Place the cod fillets on the prepared baking sheet.
4. In a small saucepan, melt the unsalted butter over medium heat.
5. Add minced garlic to the melted butter and cook for 12 minutes until fragrant.
6. Stir in chopped fresh parsley, chopped fresh chives, and lemon zest. Cook for an additional 1 minute.
7. Spoon the garlic herb butter over each cod fillet, dividing it evenly among them.
8. Bake in the preheated oven for 1215 minutes, or until the cod is cooked through and flakes easily with a fork.
9. Remove from the oven and let them cool for a minute.

10.	Serve the cod with garlic herb butter hot, with lemon wedges on the side.
11.	Enjoy the succulent cod paired with flavorful garlic herb butter for a delightful and elegant seafood dish!

Nutritional Info (per serving): Calories: 250 | Fat: 15g | Carbs: 1g | Protein: 25g

Atkins Diet Feature: This cod with garlic herb butter recipe is low in carbs and high in protein, making it suitable for the Atkins Diet. It's a simple yet elegant dish that's perfect for any occasion.

Shrimp and Veggie Kabobs

Prep: 20 mins | Cook: 10 mins | Serves: 4

Ingredients:
- 1 lb large shrimp, peeled and deveined (about 450g)
- 2 bell peppers (assorted colors), cut into chunks
- 1 red onion, cut into chunks
- 1 zucchini, sliced into rounds
- 8 cherry tomatoes
- 2 tablespoons olive oil (30ml)
- 2 cloves garlic, minced
- 1 teaspoon smoked paprika (5g)
- 1 teaspoon dried thyme (5g)
- Salt and pepper to taste
- Wooden or metal skewers

Instructions:
1. If using wooden skewers, soak them in water for at least 30 minutes to prevent them from burning.
2. In a bowl, combine peeled and deveined shrimp, bell pepper chunks, red onion chunks, zucchini slices, and cherry tomatoes.
3. In a separate small bowl, whisk together olive oil, minced garlic, smoked paprika, dried thyme, salt, and pepper.

4. Pour the olive oil mixture over the shrimp and veggies, tossing until they are evenly coated.
5. Thread the shrimp and veggies onto skewers, alternating between them.
6. Preheat your grill to mediumhigh heat.
7. Grill the skewers for 23 minutes on each side, or until the shrimp are pink and cooked through, and the veggies are tender and slightly charred.
8. Remove from the grill and let them cool for a minute.
9. Serve the shrimp and veggie kabobs hot, and enjoy this colorful and flavorful dish!

Nutritional Info (per serving): Calories: 200 | Fat: 8g | Carbs: 10g | Protein: 25g

Atkins Diet Feature: These shrimp and veggie kabobs are relatively low in carbs and high in protein, making them suitable for the Atkins Diet. They're a fun and delicious way to enjoy a variety of grilled flavors!

Crab Stuffed Mushrooms

Prep: 20 mins | Cook: 20 mins | Serves: 4

Ingredients:
- 12 large mushrooms, stems removed and caps cleaned
- 1 cup lump crab meat (100g)
- 1/4 cup almond flour (25g)
- 1/4 cup grated Parmesan cheese (25g)
- 2 tablespoons mayonnaise (30ml)
- 1 tablespoon chopped fresh parsley
- 1 teaspoon Old Bay seasoning (5g)
- Salt and pepper to taste
- Lemon wedges for serving

Instructions:

1. Preheat your oven to 375°F (190°C). Line a baking sheet with parchment paper.
2. In a mixing bowl, combine lump crab meat, almond flour, grated Parmesan cheese, mayonnaise, chopped fresh parsley, Old Bay seasoning, salt, and pepper. Mix until well combined.
3. Spoon the crab mixture into each mushroom cap, dividing it evenly among them.
4. Place the stuffed mushrooms on the prepared baking sheet.
5. Bake in the preheated oven for 1520 minutes, or until the mushrooms are tender and the filling is golden brown on top.
6. Remove from the oven and let them cool for a minute.
7. Serve the crab stuffed mushrooms hot, with lemon wedges on the side.
8. Enjoy these savory and indulgent appetizers that are perfect for parties or special occasions!

Nutritional Info (per serving): Calories: 150 | Fat: 10g | Carbs: 3g | Protein: 10g

Atkins Diet Feature: These crab stuffed mushrooms are low in carbs and high in protein, making them suitable for the Atkins Diet. They're a delicious and elegant appetizer that's sure to impress your guests!

CHAPTER EIGHT: SIDE DISHES

Cauliflower Rice

Prep: 10 mins | Cook: 10 mins | Serves: 4

Ingredients:
- 1 head cauliflower, grated
- 2 tablespoons olive oil (30ml)
- 2 cloves garlic, minced
- Salt and pepper to taste
- Fresh chopped parsley for garnish

Instructions:
1. Cut the cauliflower into florets, discarding the tough stems.
2. Working in batches, pulse the cauliflower florets in a food processor until they resemble rice grains.
3. Heat olive oil in a large skillet over medium heat.
4. Add minced garlic to the skillet and cook for 1 minute until fragrant.
5. Add the grated cauliflower to the skillet and toss to coat with the garlicinfused oil.
6. Cook the cauliflower rice for 57 minutes, stirring occasionally, until it is tender but still has a slight bite.
7. Season with salt and pepper to taste.
8. Remove from heat and let it cool for a minute.
9. Garnish with fresh chopped parsley before serving. Enjoy this versatile and lowcarb alternative to rice!

Nutritional Info (per serving): Calories: 60 | Fat: 4g | Carbs: 6g | Protein: 2g

Zucchini Noodles

Prep: 10 mins | Cook: 5 mins | Serves: 4

Ingredients:
- 4 medium zucchini
- 2 tablespoons olive oil (30ml)
- 2 cloves garlic, minced
- Salt and pepper to taste
- Fresh basil leaves for garnish

Instructions:
1. Using a spiralizer, spiralize the zucchini into noodles according to the manufacturer's instructions.
2. Heat olive oil in a large skillet over medium heat.
3. Add minced garlic to the skillet and cook for 1 minute until fragrant.
4. Add zucchini noodles to the skillet and toss with the garlicinfused oil.
5. Cook the zucchini noodles for 23 minutes, stirring occasionally, until they are just tender but still crisp.
6. Season with salt and pepper to taste.
7. Remove from heat and let them cool for a minute.
8. Serve the zucchini noodles hot, garnished with fresh basil leaves if desired. Enjoy this light and healthy alternative to pasta!

Nutritional Info (per serving): Calories: 60 | Fat: 7g | Carbs: 4g | Protein: 2g

Atkins Diet Feature: These zucchini noodles are low in carbs and packed with fiber, making them a perfect fit for the Atkins Diet. They're a satisfying and nutritious substitute for traditional pasta dishes.

Prep: 10 mins | Cook: 20 mins | Serves: 4

Ingredients:
- 1 lb broccoli florets (about 450g)
- 2 tablespoons olive oil (30ml)
- 2 cloves garlic, minced
- Salt and pepper to taste

Instructions:
1. Preheat your oven to 425°F (220°C).
2. Toss the broccoli florets with olive oil, minced garlic, salt, and pepper in a large bowl until evenly coated.
3. Spread the broccoli out in a single layer on a baking sheet.
4. Roast in the preheated oven for 1820 minutes, or until the broccoli is tender and slightly caramelized, stirring halfway through cooking.
5. Remove from the oven and let them cool for a minute.
6. Serve the roasted broccoli hot, and enjoy this simple yet delicious side dish!

Nutritional Info (per serving): Calories: 120 | Fat: 7g | Carbs: 12g | Protein: 4g

Atkins Diet Feature: Broccoli is a nutrientdense vegetable that's low in carbs and high in fiber, making it an excellent choice for the Atkins Diet. Roasting enhances its flavor and adds a satisfying crunch, making it a favorite side dish for many lowcarb enthusiasts.

Prep: 10 mins | Cook: 25 mins | Serves: 4

Ingredients:
- 1 lb Brussels sprouts, trimmed and halved (about 450g)
- 2 tablespoons olive oil (30ml)
- 2 cloves garlic, minced
- Salt and pepper to taste

Instructions:
1. Preheat your oven to 400°F (200°C).
2. Toss the Brussels sprouts with olive oil, minced garlic, salt, and pepper in a large bowl until evenly coated.
3. Spread the Brussels sprouts out in a single layer on a baking sheet.
4. Roast in the preheated oven for 2025 minutes, or until the Brussels sprouts are tender and caramelized, stirring halfway through cooking.
5. Remove from the oven and let them cool for a minute.
6. Serve the roasted Brussels sprouts hot, and enjoy this flavorful and nutritious side dish!

Nutritional Info (per serving): Calories: 90 | Fat: 7g | Carbs: 8g | Protein: 4g

Atkins Diet Feature: Brussels sprouts are a cruciferous vegetable that's packed with fiber and nutrients, making them a great choice for the Atkins Diet. Roasting them brings out their natural sweetness and creates a delicious caramelized flavor that pairs well with a variety of main dishes.

Green Beans Almondine

Prep: 10 mins | Cook: 15 mins | Serves: 4

Ingredients:
- 1 lb green beans, trimmed
- 2 tablespoons unsalted butter (30g)
- 1/4 cup sliced almonds (25g)
- 2 cloves garlic, minced
- Salt and pepper to taste
- Lemon wedges for serving

Instructions:
1. Bring a large pot of salted water to a boil.
2. Add the trimmed green beans to the boiling water and cook for 34 minutes, or until they are tender but still crisp.
3. Drain the green beans and immediately transfer them to a bowl of ice water to stop the cooking process. Drain again and set aside.
4. In a large skillet, melt the unsalted butter over medium heat.
5. Add sliced almonds to the melted butter and cook, stirring frequently, until the almonds are lightly toasted, about 23 minutes.
6. Add minced garlic to the skillet and cook for 1 minute until fragrant.
7. Add the blanched green beans to the skillet and toss until they are coated with the butter and almond mixture.
8. Drizzle lemon juice over the green beans and season with salt and pepper to taste, tossing to combine.
9. Cook for an additional 23 minutes, or until the green beans are heated through.
10. Remove from heat and let them cool for a minute.
11. Serve the green beans almondine hot, and enjoy this classic and flavorful side dish!

Nutritional Info (per serving): Calories: 140 | Fat: 10g | Carbs: 10g | Protein: 5g

Atkins Diet Feature: These green beans almondine are relatively low in carbs and high in fiber, making them suitable for the Atkins Diet. They're a delicious and nutritious accompaniment to any meal!

Creamed Spinach

Prep: 10 mins | Cook: 15 mins | Serves: 4

Ingredients:
- 1 lb fresh spinach, washed and chopped
- 2 tablespoons unsalted butter (30g)
- 2 cloves garlic, minced
- 1/4 cup heavy cream (60ml)
- 1/4 cup grated Parmesan cheese (25g)
- Salt and pepper to taste
- Pinch of nutmeg (optional)

Instructions:
1. In a large skillet, melt the unsalted butter over medium heat.
2. Add minced garlic to the melted butter and cook for 1 minute until fragrant.
3. Add the chopped spinach to the skillet and cook, stirring occasionally, until wilted, about 35 minutes.
4. Stir in heavy cream and grated Parmesan cheese until the cheese is melted and the mixture is creamy.
5. Season with salt, pepper, and a pinch of nutmeg if desired, stirring to combine.
6. Cook for an additional 23 minutes, or until the creamed spinach is heated through.
7. Remove from heat and let it cool for a minute.
8. Serve the creamed spinach hot, and enjoy this rich and creamy side dish!

Nutritional Info (per serving): Calories: 150 | Fat: 12g | Carbs: 4g | Protein: 6g

Atkins Diet Feature: Creamed spinach is a ketofriendly side dish, rich in healthy fats and low in carbs, making it suitable for the Atkins Diet. It's a comforting and flavorful addition to any meal.

Fried Cabbage

Prep: 10 mins | Cook: 15 mins | Serves: 4

Ingredients:
- 1 head cabbage, shredded
- 4 slices bacon, chopped
- 1 onion, thinly sliced
- 2 cloves garlic, minced
- Salt and pepper to taste
- Chopped fresh parsley for garnish

Instructions:
1. In a large skillet, cook the chopped bacon over medium heat until crispy.
2. Remove the bacon from the skillet and set aside, leaving the bacon drippings in the pan.
3. Add thinly sliced onion to the skillet and cook in the bacon drippings until softened and translucent.
4. Add minced garlic to the skillet and cook for 1 minute until fragrant.
5. Add the shredded cabbage to the skillet and toss to combine with the onions and garlic.
6. Cook the cabbage mixture for 810 minutes, stirring occasionally, until it is tender but still retains some crispness.
7. Season with salt and pepper to taste.
8. Stir in the cooked bacon pieces.
9. Remove from heat and let it cool for a minute.
10. Serve the fried cabbage hot, garnished with chopped fresh parsley if desired. Enjoy this savory and comforting side dish!

Nutritional Info (per serving): Calories: 120 | Fat: 7g | Carbs: 10g | Protein: 4g

Atkins Diet Feature: This fried cabbage is relatively low in carbs and pairs well with proteinrich main dishes, making it a suitable option for the Atkins Diet. It's a flavorful and hearty side dish that's quick and easy to prepare.

Garlic Parmesan Asparagus

Prep: 10 mins | Cook: 15 mins | Serves: 4

Ingredients:
- 1 bunch asparagus, tough ends trimmed (about 1 lb or 450g)
- 2 tablespoons olive oil (30ml)
- 2 cloves garlic, minced
- 1/4 cup grated Parmesan cheese (25g)
- Salt and pepper to taste
- Lemon wedges for serving

Instructions:
1. Preheat your oven to 425°F (220°C).
2. Place the trimmed asparagus on a baking sheet.
3. Drizzle olive oil over the asparagus, then sprinkle minced garlic, grated Parmesan cheese, salt, and pepper evenly.
4. Toss the asparagus until evenly coated with the seasoning.
5. Spread the asparagus out in a single layer on the baking sheet.
6. Roast in the preheated oven for 1215 minutes, or until the asparagus is tender and the Parmesan cheese is golden brown and crispy.
7. Remove from the oven and let them cool for a minute.
8. Serve the garlic Parmesan asparagus hot, with lemon wedges on the side.
9. Enjoy this flavorful and nutritious side dish!

Nutritional Info (per serving): Calories: 90 | Fat: 7g | Carbs: 4g | Protein: 4g

Atkins Diet Feature: This dish is low in carbs and high in flavor, making it perfect for the Atkins Diet. The combination of garlic, Parmesan, and asparagus provides a delicious and satisfying side for any meal.

Veggie Kabobs

Prep: 20 mins | Cook: 10 mins | Serves: 4

Ingredients:
- 2 bell peppers (assorted colors), cut into chunks
- 1 red onion, cut into chunks
- 1 zucchini, sliced into rounds
- 8 cherry tomatoes
- 8 button mushrooms
- 2 tablespoons olive oil (30ml)
- 2 cloves garlic, minced
- 1 teaspoon dried oregano (5g)
- Salt and pepper to taste
- Wooden or metal skewers

Instructions:
1. If using wooden skewers, soak them in water for at least 30 minutes to prevent burning.
2. Thread the bell peppers, red onion, zucchini, cherry tomatoes, and mushrooms onto skewers, alternating between them.
3. In a small bowl, mix olive oil, minced garlic, dried oregano, salt, and pepper.
4. Brush the olive oil mixture over the skewered veggies, coating them evenly.
5. Preheat your grill to mediumhigh heat.
6. Grill the veggie kabobs for 34 minutes on each side, or until they are tender and lightly charred.
7. Remove from the grill and let them cool for a minute.
8. Serve the veggie kabobs hot, and enjoy this colorful and flavorful side dish!

Nutritional Info (per serving): Calories: 100 | Fat: 7g | Carbs: 8g | Protein: 3g

Atkins Diet Feature: These veggie kabobs are a carbconscious option that's bursting with flavor. Grilling brings out the natural sweetness of the vegetables, making them a delightful addition to your Atkinsfriendly meals.

Roasted Cauliflower

Prep: 10 mins | Cook: 25 mins | Serves: 4

Ingredients:
- 1 head cauliflower, cut into florets
- 2 tablespoons olive oil (30ml)
- 2 cloves garlic, minced
- 1 teaspoon smoked paprika (5g)
- Salt and pepper to taste
- Fresh chopped parsley for garnish

Instructions:
1. Preheat your oven to 425°F (220°C) and line a baking sheet with parchment paper.
2. In a large bowl, toss cauliflower florets with olive oil, minced garlic, smoked paprika, salt, and pepper until evenly coated.
3. Spread the cauliflower florets out in a single layer on the prepared baking sheet.
4. Roast in the preheated oven for 2025 minutes, or until the cauliflower is golden brown and tender, tossing halfway through cooking.
5. Remove from the oven and let it cool for a minute.
6. Transfer the roasted cauliflower to a serving dish, garnish with fresh chopped parsley, and serve hot. Enjoy this simple and flavorful side dish!

Nutritional Info (per serving): Calories: 90 | Fat: 7g | Carbs: 6g | Protein: 3g

Atkins Diet Feature: This roasted cauliflower is low in carbs and high in fiber, making it a great choice for the Atkins Diet. It's a versatile side dish that pairs well with a variety of main courses.

Cheesy Cauliflower Tots

Prep: 15 mins | Cook: 25 mins | Serves: 4

Ingredients:
- 1 medium head cauliflower, grated (about 4 cups)
- 1/2 cup grated cheddar cheese (50g)
- 1/4 cup almond flour (30g)
- 1 egg, beaten
- 2 tablespoons chopped fresh parsley
- Salt and pepper to taste
- Cooking spray

Instructions:
1. Preheat your oven to 400°F (200°C) and grease a baking sheet with cooking spray.
2. In a large bowl, combine the grated cauliflower, grated cheddar cheese, almond flour, beaten egg, chopped fresh parsley, salt, and pepper. Mix well until thoroughly combined.
3. Using your hands, shape the cauliflower mixture into small tots and place them on the prepared baking sheet.
4. Bake in the preheated oven for 2025 minutes, or until the tots are golden brown and crispy, flipping halfway through cooking.
5. Remove from the oven and let them cool for a minute.
6. Serve the cheesy cauliflower tots hot, and enjoy this tasty and lowcarb alternative to traditional tater tots!

Nutritional Info (per serving): Calories: 120 | Fat: 7g | Carbs: 6g | Protein: 8g

Atkins Diet Feature: These cheesy cauliflower tots are low in carbs and high in protein, making them suitable for the Atkins Diet. They're a delicious and satisfying side dish or snack option!

Prep: 10 mins | Cook: 25 mins | Serves: 4

Ingredients:
- 1 lb Brussels sprouts, trimmed and halved
- 4 slices bacon, chopped
- 2 tablespoons olive oil (30ml)
- 2 cloves garlic, minced
- Salt and pepper to taste

Instructions:
1. Preheat your oven to 400°F (200°C) and line a baking sheet with parchment paper.
2. In a large skillet, cook the chopped bacon over medium heat until crispy.
3. Remove the bacon from the skillet and set aside, leaving the bacon drippings in the pan.
4. Add halved Brussels sprouts to the skillet with the bacon drippings and toss to coat.
5. Transfer the Brussels sprouts to the prepared baking sheet, spreading them out in a single layer.
6. Drizzle olive oil over the Brussels sprouts and sprinkle minced garlic, salt, and pepper evenly.
7. Toss the Brussels sprouts until they are evenly coated with the seasonings.
8. Roast in the preheated oven for 2025 minutes, or until the Brussels sprouts are tender and caramelized, stirring halfway through cooking.
9. Remove from the oven and let them cool for a minute.
10. Sprinkle the cooked bacon over the roasted Brussels sprouts before serving. Enjoy this flavorful and satisfying side dish!

Nutritional Info (per serving): Calories: 150 | Fat: 10g | Carbs: 10g | Protein: 6g

Atkins Diet Feature: These bacon Brussels sprouts are low in carbs and high in flavor, making them a great

choice for the Atkins Diet. They're a delicious way to incorporate vegetables into your meals while still enjoying the savory goodness of bacon.

Creamed Kale

Prep: 10 mins | Cook: 15 mins | Serves: 4

Ingredients:
- 1 lb kale, stems removed and leaves chopped
- 2 tablespoons unsalted butter (30g)
- 2 cloves garlic, minced
- 1/2 cup heavy cream (120ml)
- 1/4 cup grated Parmesan cheese (25g)
- Salt and pepper to taste
- Pinch of nutmeg (optional)

Instructions:
1. In a large skillet, melt the unsalted butter over medium heat.
2. Add minced garlic to the melted butter and cook for 1 minute until fragrant.
3. Add the chopped kale to the skillet and cook, stirring occasionally, until wilted, about 57 minutes.
4. Stir in heavy cream and grated Parmesan cheese until the cheese is melted and the mixture is creamy.
5. Season with salt, pepper, and a pinch of nutmeg if desired, stirring to combine.
6. Cook for an additional 23 minutes, or until the creamed kale is heated through.
7. Remove from heat and let it cool for a minute.
8. Serve the creamed kale hot, and enjoy this rich and nutritious side dish!

Nutritional Info (per serving): Calories: 150 | Fat: 10g | Carbs: 7g | Protein: 6g

Atkins Diet Feature: This creamed kale is low in carbs and high in fat, making it suitable for the Atkins Diet. It's a comforting and flavorful side dish that pairs well with any protein!

Parmesan Tomato Zucchini Boats

Prep: 15 mins | Cook: 25 mins | Serves: 4

Ingredients:
- 2 large zucchinis
- 1 cup cherry tomatoes, halved
- 1/4 cup grated Parmesan cheese (25g)
- 2 tablespoons olive oil (30ml)
- 2 cloves garlic, minced
- Salt and pepper to taste
- Fresh basil leaves for garnish

Instructions:
1. Preheat your oven to 375°F (190°C) and line a baking dish with parchment paper.
2. Cut the zucchinis in half lengthwise and scoop out the seeds and flesh to create "boats".
3. In a bowl, combine the cherry tomatoes, grated Parmesan cheese, olive oil, minced garlic, salt, and pepper.
4. Stuff each zucchini boat with the tomato mixture.
5. Place the stuffed zucchini boats in the prepared baking dish.
6. Bake in the preheated oven for 2025 minutes, or until the zucchinis are tender and the filling is heated through.
7. Remove from the oven and let them cool for a minute.
8. Garnish with fresh basil leaves before serving. Enjoy this colorful and flavorful side dish!

Nutritional Info (per serving): Calories: 100 | Fat: 7g | Carbs: 6g | Protein: 3g

Atkins Diet Feature: These Parmesan tomato zucchini boats are low in carbs and packed with flavor, making them a great choice for the Atkins Diet. They're a delicious and healthy way to enjoy seasonal produce!

Prep: 15 mins | Cook: 30 mins | Serves: 4

Ingredients:
- 4 medium zucchinis, thinly sliced
- 1 cup shredded mozzarella cheese (100g)
- 1/4 cup grated Parmesan cheese (25g)
- 1/4 cup heavy cream (60ml)
- 2 cloves garlic, minced
- 2 tablespoons unsalted butter (30g)
- Salt and pepper to taste
- Fresh chopped parsley for garnish

Instructions:
1. Preheat your oven to 375°F (190°C) and grease a baking dish with butter or cooking spray.
2. In a skillet, melt the unsalted butter over medium heat.
3. Add minced garlic to the melted butter and cook for 1 minute until fragrant.
4. Add the thinly sliced zucchinis to the skillet and cook for 34 minutes, or until they are just tender.
5. Season the zucchinis with salt and pepper to taste.
6. In a small bowl, mix together the shredded mozzarella cheese, grated Parmesan cheese, and heavy cream.
7. Arrange half of the cooked zucchini slices in the bottom of the prepared baking dish.
8. Spread half of the cheese mixture over the zucchinis.
9. Repeat the layers with the remaining zucchini slices and cheese mixture.
10. Bake in the preheated oven for 2025 minutes, or until the cheese is bubbly and golden brown.
11. Remove from the oven and let it cool for a minute.
12. Garnish with fresh chopped parsley before serving. Enjoy this creamy and indulgent side dish!

Nutritional Info (per serving): Calories: 200 | Fat: 15g | Carbs: 6g | Protein: 10g

Atkins Diet Feature: This cheesy zucchini gratin is low in carbs and high in fat, making it a satisfying option for the Atkins Diet. It's a decadent and comforting way to enjoy zucchini!

CHAPTER NINE: DESERTS

Mixed Berry Yogurt Bark

Prep: 10 mins | Cook: 3 hours | Serves: 6

Ingredients:
- 2 cups Greek yogurt (480g)
- 1 cup mixed berries (strawberries, blueberries, raspberries) (150g)
- 2 tablespoons honey or lowcarb sweetener (30ml)
- 1 teaspoon vanilla extract (5ml)

Instructions:
1. Line a baking sheet with parchment paper.
2. In a bowl, mix Greek yogurt, honey, and vanilla extract.
3. Spread the yogurt mixture evenly onto the prepared baking sheet.
4. Sprinkle mixed berries over the yogurt mixture.
5. Freeze for at least 3 hours or until solid.
6. Once frozen, break the bark into pieces.
7. Serve immediately or store in the freezer in an airtight container.

Nutritional Info (per serving): Calories: 90 | Fat: 0g | Carbs: 12g | Protein: 9g

Atkins Diet Feature: Low in carbs and high in protein, this Mixed Berry Yogurt Bark is a satisfying dessert option that satisfies sweet cravings without derailing ketosis.

Chocolate Chia Pudding

Prep: 5 mins | Cook: 3 hours | Serves: 4

Ingredients:
- 1 cup unsweetened almond milk (240ml)
- 1/4 cup chia seeds (40g)
- 2 tablespoons unsweetened cocoa powder (15g)
- 2 tablespoons lowcarb sweetener (30ml)
- 1/2 teaspoon vanilla extract (2.5ml)

Instructions:
1. In a bowl, whisk together almond milk, cocoa powder, sweetener, and vanilla extract.
2. Stir in chia seeds until well combined.
3. Let the mixture sit for 5 minutes, then whisk again to break up any clumps.
4. Cover and refrigerate for at least 3 hours or overnight until thickened.
5. Stir well before serving and adjust sweetness to taste if necessary.
6. Serve chilled with your favorite toppings such as berries or nuts.

Nutritional Info (per serving): Calories: 70 | Fat: 4g | Carbs: 8g | Protein: 3g

Atkins Diet Feature: Rich in fiber and low in net carbs, Chocolate Chia Pudding is a decadent dessert that supports ketosis while providing essential nutrients.

Coconut Fat Bombs

Prep: 10 mins | Cook: 1 hour | Serves: 12

Ingredients:
- 1/2 cup coconut oil, melted (120ml)
- 1/4 cup unsweetened shredded coconut (20g)
- 2 tablespoons almond butter (30g)
- 2 tablespoons unsweetened cocoa powder (15g)
- 1 tablespoon lowcarb sweetener (15ml)
- 1/2 teaspoon vanilla extract (2.5ml)

Instructions:
1. In a bowl, mix melted coconut oil, almond butter, cocoa powder, sweetener, and vanilla extract until smooth.
2. Stir in shredded coconut until well combined.
3. Spoon the mixture into silicone molds or mini muffin cups.
4. Freeze for 1 hour or until firm.
5. Remove from molds and store in an airtight container in the refrigerator.

Nutritional Info (per serving): Calories: 90 | Fat: 9g | Carbs: 2g | Protein: 1g

Atkins Diet Feature: These Coconut Fat Bombs are a convenient way to boost fat intake on the Atkins Diet. With only 2g of net carbs per serving, they satisfy cravings while supporting ketosis.

Peanut Butter Fudge

Prep: 10 mins | Cook: 1 hour | Serves: 9

Ingredients:
- 1/2 cup natural peanut butter (120g)
- 1/4 cup coconut oil, melted (60ml)
- 2 tablespoons lowcarb sweetener (30ml)
- 1 teaspoon vanilla extract (5ml)
- Pinch of salt

Instructions:
1. Line a small baking dish with parchment paper.
2. In a microwavesafe bowl, mix peanut butter, melted coconut oil, sweetener, vanilla extract, and salt until smooth.
3. Pour the mixture into the prepared baking dish and spread evenly.
4. Refrigerate for at least 1 hour or until firm.
5. Cut into squares and serve chilled.

Nutritional Info (per serving): Calories: 160 | Fat: 15g | Carbs: 3g | Protein: 4g

Atkins Diet Feature: This Peanut Butter Fudge is a delicious treat that's low in carbs and high in healthy fats, making it suitable for the Atkins Diet. Enjoy a satisfying indulgence without compromising ketosis.

Cheesecake Mousse

Prep: 10 mins | Cook: 0 mins | Serves: 4

Ingredients:
- 8 oz cream cheese, softened (225g)
- 1/4 cup heavy cream (60ml)
- 2 tablespoons lowcarb sweetener (30ml)
- 1 teaspoon vanilla extract (5ml)
- Lemon zest for garnish (optional)

Instructions:
1. In a bowl, beat softened cream cheese until smooth and creamy.
2. Add heavy cream, sweetener, and vanilla extract, and beat until well combined and fluffy.
3. Divide the mixture into serving glasses.
4. Refrigerate for at least 1 hour or until chilled and set.
5. Garnish with lemon zest before serving if desired.

Nutritional Info (per serving): Calories: 280 | Fat: 27g | Carbs: 3g | Protein: 5g

Atkins Diet Feature: This Cheesecake Mousse is a luscious dessert option that's low in carbs and high in fat, perfect for satisfying sweet cravings while following the Atkins Diet.

Lemon Bars

Prep: 15 mins | Cook: 25 mins | Serves: 9

Ingredients:
- 1 cup almond flour (120g)
- 1/4 cup coconut flour (30g)
- 1/4 cup lowcarb sweetener (60ml)
- 1/2 cup unsalted butter, melted (120g)
- 4 large eggs
- 1/2 cup fresh lemon juice (120ml)
- Zest of 1 lemon
- 1/4 cup powdered lowcarb sweetener, for dusting (30ml)

Instructions:
1. Preheat your oven to 350°F (175°C) and grease a square baking dish.
2. In a bowl, combine almond flour, coconut flour, and 1/4 cup of lowcarb sweetener. Mix well.
3. Add melted butter to the flour mixture and stir until a dough forms.
4. Press the dough evenly into the bottom of the prepared baking dish.
5. Bake the crust in the preheated oven for 1012 minutes, or until lightly golden.
6. In another bowl, whisk together eggs, lemon juice, lemon zest, and powdered lowcarb sweetener until well combined.
7. Pour the lemon mixture over the baked crust.
8. Return the baking dish to the oven and bake for an additional 1518 minutes, or until the filling is set.
9. Allow the lemon bars to cool completely in the baking dish.
10. Once cooled, dust the top with powdered lowcarb sweetener.
11. Cut into squares and serve.

Nutritional Info (per serving): Calories: 180 | Fat: 15g | Carbs: 5g | Protein: 5g

Atkins Diet Feature: These lemon bars are made with almond and coconut flour, making them low in carbs and suitable for the Atkins Diet. They offer a refreshing and tangy dessert option.

Chocolate Mug Cake

Prep: 5 mins | Cook: 1 min | Serves: 1

Ingredients:
- 2 tablespoons almond flour (15g)
- 1 tablespoon unsweetened cocoa powder (5g)
- 1 tablespoon lowcarb sweetener (15ml)
- 1/4 teaspoon baking powder (1.25ml)
- 1 tablespoon unsalted butter, melted (15g)
- 1 large egg
- 1/4 teaspoon vanilla extract (1.25ml)
- Whipped cream for topping (optional)

Instructions:
1. In a microwavesafe mug, mix almond flour, cocoa powder, lowcarb sweetener, and baking powder.
2. Add melted butter, egg, and vanilla extract to the dry ingredients. Stir until well combined.
3. Microwave on high for 6090 seconds, or until the cake is set.
4. Let the mug cake cool for a minute before serving.
5. Top with whipped cream if desired.

Nutritional Info (per serving): Calories: 250 | Fat: 20g | Carbs: 5g | Protein: 8g

Atkins Diet Feature: This Chocolate Mug Cake is a quick and easy dessert option that's low in carbs and high in fat, making it perfect for the Atkins Diet. It's a satisfying treat for one!

Chocolate Avocado Mousse

Prep: 10 mins | Cook: 0 mins | Serves: 4

Ingredients:
- 2 ripe avocados, peeled and pitted
- 1/4 cup unsweetened cocoa powder (20g)
- 1/4 cup lowcarb sweetener (60ml)
- 1/4 cup unsweetened almond milk (60ml)
- 1 teaspoon vanilla extract (5ml)

Instructions:
1. In a food processor or blender, combine avocados, cocoa powder, lowcarb sweetener, almond milk, and vanilla extract.
2. Blend until smooth and creamy, scraping down the sides as needed.
3. Taste and adjust sweetness if necessary.
4. Transfer the mousse to serving bowls or glasses.
5. Chill in the refrigerator for at least 30 minutes before serving.
6. Garnish with shaved chocolate or berries if desired.

Nutritional Info (per serving): Calories: 200 | Fat: 15g | Carbs: 10g | Protein: 3g

Atkins Diet Feature: This Chocolate Avocado Mousse is a rich and creamy dessert option that's low in carbs and packed with healthy fats from avocados. It's a decadent treat that satisfies sweet cravings while following the Atkins Diet.

Strawberry Smoothie Pops

Prep: 10 mins | Cook: 4 hours | Serves: 6

Ingredients:
- 2 cups strawberries, hulled (300g)
- 1 cup unsweetened almond milk (240ml)

- 1/4 cup lowcarb sweetener (60ml)
- 1 teaspoon vanilla extract (5ml)

Instructions:
1. In a blender, combine strawberries, almond milk, lowcarb sweetener, and vanilla extract.
2. Blend until smooth.
3. Pour the mixture into popsicle molds.
4. Insert popsicle sticks into the molds.
5. Freeze for at least 4 hours or until solid.
6. Remove the popsicles from the molds by running them under warm water.
7. Serve immediately and enjoy a refreshing and fruity treat!

Nutritional Info (per serving): Calories: 40 | Fat: 1g | Carbs: 7g | Protein: 1g

Atkins Diet Feature: These Strawberry Smoothie Pops are a delightful lowcarb dessert option that's perfect for hot days. They're packed with fresh fruit flavor and are sure to satisfy your sweet tooth while following the Atkins Diet.

Protein Energy Bites

Prep: 10 mins | Cook: 0 mins | Serves: 12

Ingredients:
- 1 cup almond flour (120g)
- 1/4 cup vanilla protein powder (30g)
- 1/4 cup almond butter (60g)
- 2 tablespoons lowcarb sweetener (30ml)
- 2 tablespoons unsweetened almond milk (30ml)
- 1 teaspoon vanilla extract (5ml)
- 1/4 cup sugarfree chocolate chips (45g)

Instructions:
1. In a mixing bowl, combine almond flour, protein powder, almond butter, lowcarb sweetener, almond milk, and vanilla extract.
2. Mix until well combined and a dough forms.
3. Fold in sugarfree chocolate chips.
4. Roll the dough into small balls using your hands.
5. Place the energy bites on a baking sheet lined with parchment paper.
6. Chill in the refrigerator for at least 30 minutes before serving.
7. Enjoy these proteinpacked bites as a satisfying dessert or snack!

Nutritional Info (per serving): Calories: 90 | Fat: 7g | Carbs: 3g | Protein: 5g

Atkins Diet Feature: These Protein Energy Bites are a convenient and nutritious dessert option that's low in carbs and high in protein. They're perfect for satisfying cravings and providing a quick energy boost while following the Atkins Diet.

Chocolate Coconut Haystacks

Prep: 10 mins | Cook: 0 mins | Serves: 10

Ingredients:
- 1 cup unsweetened shredded coconut (75g)
- 1/4 cup coconut oil, melted (60ml)
- 2 tablespoons unsweetened cocoa powder (15g)
- 2 tablespoons lowcarb sweetener (30ml)
- 1/2 teaspoon vanilla extract (2.5ml)
- Pinch of salt

Instructions:
1. In a mixing bowl, combine shredded coconut, melted coconut oil, cocoa powder, lowcarb sweetener, vanilla extract, and a pinch of salt.
2. Stir until well combined and the coconut is evenly coated.
3. Drop spoonfuls of the mixture onto a baking sheet lined with parchment paper.
4. Chill in the refrigerator for 30 minutes or until set.

5. Once set, store the haystacks in an airtight container in the refrigerator.
6. Enjoy these chocolatey coconut treats whenever you need a sweet fix!

Nutritional Info (per serving): Calories: 90 | Fat: 9g | Carbs: 2g | Protein: 1g

Atkins Diet Feature: These Chocolate Coconut Haystacks are a deliciously indulgent dessert option that's low in carbs and high in healthy fats. They're easy to make and perfect for satisfying sweet cravings while following the Atkins Diet.

Coconut Macaroons

Prep: 10 mins | Cook: 20 mins | Serves: 12

Ingredients:
- 2 cups unsweetened shredded coconut (150g)
- 1/4 cup coconut flour (30g)
- 1/4 cup lowcarb sweetener (60ml)
- 3 large egg whites
- 1 teaspoon vanilla extract (5ml)
- Pinch of salt

Instructions:
1. Preheat your oven to 325°F (160°C) and line a baking sheet with parchment paper.
2. In a mixing bowl, combine shredded coconut, coconut flour, lowcarb sweetener, vanilla extract, and a pinch of salt.
3. In a separate bowl, beat egg whites until stiff peaks form.
4. Gently fold the beaten egg whites into the coconut mixture until well combined.
5. Using a spoon or cookie scoop, portion the mixture into mounds on the prepared baking sheet.
6. Bake in the preheated oven for 1820 minutes, or until the macaroons are lightly golden.
7. Allow the macaroons to cool on the baking sheet for a few minutes before transferring them to a wire rack to cool completely.

8. Once cooled, store the macaroons in an airtight container at room temperature.
9. Enjoy these chewy and coconutty treats as a delightful dessert or snack!

Nutritional Info (per serving): Calories: 90 | Fat: 7g | Carbs: 4g | Protein: 2g

Atkins Diet Feature: These Coconut Macaroons are a classic dessert option that's low in carbs and perfect for satisfying sweet cravings while following the Atkins Diet. They're easy to make and wonderfully delicious!

Pumpkin Pie Mousse

Prep: 10 mins | Cook: 0 mins | Serves: 4

Ingredients:

1 cup canned pumpkin puree (240g)

1/2 cup heavy cream (120ml)

1/4 cup lowcarb sweetener (60ml)

1 teaspoon pumpkin pie spice (5ml)

1/2 teaspoon vanilla extract (2.5ml)

Whipped cream for topping (optional)

Ground cinnamon for garnish (optional)

Instructions:
1. In a mixing bowl, combine pumpkin puree, heavy cream, lowcarb sweetener, pumpkin pie spice, and vanilla extract.
2. Using a hand mixer or stand mixer, beat the mixture until thick and creamy.
3. Taste and adjust sweetness or spice if desired.
4. Divide the pumpkin mousse among serving cups or bowls.
5. Chill in the refrigerator for at least 30 minutes before serving.
6. Top with whipped cream and a sprinkle of ground cinnamon if desired.

7. Enjoy this creamy and indulgent pumpkin dessert!

Nutritional Info (per serving): Calories: 120 | Fat: 10g | Carbs: 6g | Protein: 1g

Atkins Diet Feature: This Pumpkin Pie Mousse is a deliciously creamy dessert option that's low in carbs and bursting with fall flavors. It's a satisfying treat that's perfect for enjoying while following the Atkins Diet.

Pecan Shortbread Cookies

Prep: 15 mins | Cook: 15 mins | Serves: 12

Ingredients:
- 1 cup almond flour (120g)
- 1/4 cup lowcarb sweetener (60ml)
- 1/2 cup unsalted butter, softened (120g)
- 1/4 teaspoon vanilla extract (1.25ml)
- 1/2 cup chopped pecans (60g)

Instructions:
1. Preheat your oven to 350°F (175°C) and line a baking sheet with parchment paper.
2. In a mixing bowl, cream together almond flour, lowcarb sweetener, softened butter, and vanilla extract until smooth.
3. Fold in chopped pecans until evenly distributed.
4. Scoop tablespoonsized portions of dough and roll them into balls.
5. Place the dough balls onto the prepared baking sheet and gently flatten them with the palm of your hand or a fork.
6. Bake in the preheated oven for 1215 minutes, or until the edges are golden brown.
7. Allow the cookies to cool on the baking sheet for a few minutes before transferring them to a wire rack to cool completely.
8. Once cooled, store the cookies in an airtight container at room temperature.
9. Enjoy these buttery and nutty cookies as a delightful dessert or snack!

Nutritional Info (per serving): Calories: 120 | Fat: 12g | Carbs: 2g | Protein: 2g

Atkins Diet Feature: These Pecan Shortbread Cookies are a delightful treat that's low in carbs and perfect for satisfying sweet cravings while following the Atkins Diet. They're easy to make and wonderfully delicious!

Blackberry Almond Crackers

Prep: 10 mins | Cook: 30 mins | Serves: 6

Ingredients:
- 1 cup almond flour (120g)
- 1/4 cup blackberries, mashed (60g)
- 1 tablespoon coconut oil, melted (15ml)
- 1 tablespoon lowcarb sweetener (15ml)
- 1/2 teaspoon vanilla extract (2.5ml)
- Pinch of salt

Instructions:
1. Preheat your oven to 325°F (160°C) and line a baking sheet with parchment paper.
2. In a mixing bowl, combine almond flour, mashed blackberries, melted coconut oil, lowcarb sweetener, vanilla extract, and a pinch of salt.
3. Mix until a dough forms. If the dough is too dry, you can add a little water or almond milk to achieve the right consistency.
4. Place the dough between two sheets of parchment paper and roll it out into a thin layer, about 1/8 inch thick.
5. Use a knife or pizza cutter to cut the dough into crackersized squares or rectangles.
6. Carefully transfer the cut crackers to the prepared baking sheet, spacing them apart.
7. Bake in the preheated oven for 2530 minutes, or until the crackers are firm and golden brown around the edges.
8. Remove from the oven and let the crackers cool completely on the baking sheet.

9. Once cooled, break the crackers apart along the scored lines.
10. Store the blackberry almond crackers in an airtight container at room temperature for up to one week.
11. Enjoy these homemade crackers as a tasty and nutritious snack!

Nutritional Info (per serving): Calories: 110 | Fat: 9g | Carbs: 5g | Protein: 4g

Atkins Diet Feature: These Blackberry Almond Crackers are a delicious and satisfying snack option that's perfect for the Atkins Diet. They're made with almond flour and fresh blackberries, providing a good source of healthy fats and fiber. Enjoy them on their own or with your favorite lowcarb dip or spread.

Conclusion:

Embracing a Transformative Journey

As we reach the conclusion of our exploration into the Atkins Diet, it becomes evident that this revolutionary approach to nutrition offers far more than just a means to shed unwanted pounds. It represents a transformative journey – a path towards holistic wellness, selfdiscovery, and a profound appreciation for the nourishing power of whole, minimally processed foods.

Throughout this comprehensive guide, we've delved into the intricacies of the Atkins Diet, unveiling its unique phases, the groundbreaking concept of net carbs, and the comprehensive food lists that serve as our roadmap to success. But beyond the practical guidelines and dietary recommendations, we've also explored the profound impact this lifestyle can have on our physical, mental, and emotional wellbeing.

For many of us, embarking on the Atkins Diet was initially driven by a desire for weight loss or improved health. However, as we navigated through the phases, we discovered that this journey offered so much more than just a slimmer physique or improved biomarkers. It challenged us to reevaluate our relationship with food, to embrace a more mindful and intentional approach to nourishing our bodies.

As we transitioned through the induction phase, kickstarting the process of ketosis and experiencing the rapid results, we learned the value of patience, perseverance, and selfdiscipline. We discovered that by adhering to the principles of a lowcarb, highfat way of eating, we could not only achieve our weight goals but also experience a heightened sense of mental clarity, improved energy levels, and a newfound zest for life.

The ongoing weight loss phase taught us the importance of flexibility and adaptability. By gradually reintroducing nutrientdense, lowcarb foods into our diets, we learned to listen to our bodies' cues and find our personal carbohydrate tolerance levels. This phase empowered us to craft delectable meals that not only satisfied our cravings but also supported our continued progress towards our desired outcomes.

As we entered the premaintenance and lifetime maintenance phases, we truly embraced the transformative power of the Atkins Diet. We learned to cultivate a sustainable, balanced approach to lowcarb living, prioritizing nutrientdense, whole foods while allowing for occasional indulgences in moderation. This phase taught us that the Atkins Diet is not a temporary fix but rather a lifelong journey towards holistic wellness.

Throughout this incredible journey, the concept of net carbs emerged as a gamechanger, revolutionizing our understanding of carbohydrate consumption. By focusing on the net carb content of foods – the total carbohydrates minus the fiber – we unlocked a world of culinary possibilities, embracing the rich flavors and textures of nutrientdense, fiberrich foods without compromising our commitment to a lowcarb lifestyle.

As we reflect on the lessons learned and the triumphs achieved, it becomes clear that the Atkins Diet is more than just a dietary approach; it's a catalyst for personal growth, selfdiscovery, and a deeper appreciation for the nourishing power of whole, minimally processed foods.

Moving forward, let us carry the wisdom and insights gained from this transformative journey into our daily lives. Let us continue to prioritize nutrientdensity, embrace the concept of net carbs, and cultivate a mindful, balanced approach to our culinary adventures. And above all, let us remember that true wellness is a harmonious symphony, where physical, mental, and emotional wellbeing converge in perfect harmony.

Embrace the journey, savor the flavors, and nourish your body, mind, and soul with each delicious bite. For in the end, the Atkins Diet is not merely a means to an end but a lifelong celebration of health, vitality, and the boundless potential that lies within each of us.

Printed in Great Britain
by Amazon